MASTERING EXECUTIVE
TRANSITIONS

MASTERING EXECUTIVE TRANSITIONS

THE DEFINITIVE GUIDE

NAVID NAZEMIAN, PCC

NEW DEGREE PRESS

MASTERING EXECUTIVE TRANSITIONS

The Definitive Guide

ISBN   978-1-63730-813-4   *Paperback*

             978-1-63730-875-2   *Kindle Ebook*

             978-1-63730-975-9   *Ebook*

To fellow executives who are leaving behind a leadership legacy that inspires many, and far extends their tenure:
This book is for you.

To fellow coaches who are supporting executives during critical transitions:
This book is for you.

To fellow HR leaders who are identifying, hiring, and developing exceptional executive talent:
This book is for you.

To my family who are the bedrock of a strong and stable social network:
This book is for you.

CONTENTS

———

"It is when we are in transition that we are most completely alive."

—WILLIAM BRIDGES

INTRODUCTION

———

Most people think or believe executive transitions are absolutely doable and there are plenty of processes and guidance available for executives going through a transition by their organizations. It would be fair to assume organizations have invested heavily in their executive onboarding and transition processes, and in any case if the best leader is hired, they are smart enough to make their onboarding and transition work.

However, 40 percent of all executives are pushed out, fail, or quit during their first eighteen months in a role (Keller and Meaney 2018).

Let's imagine you have just signed your new contract (or received confirmation of your appointment if you are based in the USA) for that executive position. Congratulations! It feels exciting to embark on a new chapter of your executive journey. At the same time, you have that 40 percent figure in the back of your mind. How can you avoid being part of that 40 percent club?

Let me help. Through this book, I will share strategies and tactics to elegantly and confidently achieve the following:

- De-risk your executive transition
- Substantially reduce the likelihood of derailment
- Significantly reduce your time to become productive

CURRENT STATE

When companies announce their CEOs are leaving, they often offer any number of vague reasons. Rarely would they ever say the chief executive was "fired" and explain precisely why. One study from Exechange news, who determine the so called "Push-out Score," suggests that from 2018–2020, 52 percent of announced CEO departures from companies on the Russell 3000 Index were the result of executives being shown the door (Exechange, 2020). That includes those who say they resigned, stepped down, just felt the time was "right to leave" or had a sudden urge to spend more time with their family. So, it becomes clear CEOs often have to justify their sudden departure by providing all sorts of creative explanations. As we can see, the 40 percent failure rate doesn't stop at the CEO's corner office.

McKinsey cites several research papers suggesting two years after executive transitions, between 27 percent and 46 percent are regarded as "failures or disappointments" (Keller and Meaney 2018).

Leaders rank organizational politics as the main challenge, and 67 percent of leaders wish they had moved faster to change the culture; hence, Dr. Marshall Goldsmith's advice seems fully applicable to executive transitions: "What got you here, won't get you there" (Goldsmith 2008). So, past accomplishments don't always predict future success. Bearing in mind all of the above studies, we can see nearly half of all executive transitions fail. With more and more executives facing shorter tenure in the role, this issue is like a bubble that is going to burst in the foreseeable future. Bearing all this in mind, more and more executives are going to fail and be given increasingly shorter tenures in the role, almost like a slow-motion of a snowball that is gaining traction. The war for talent may have never really ended, but looking at this scenario and its implications of an ever more competitive talent market can pose real threats to organizations.

WHY WRITE THIS BOOK, NOW

The pace and magnitude of change are constantly rising in the business world. It comes as no surprise executive transitions are increasingly common. There is a very practical and pressing need for organizations to safeguard their investments in sourcing and onboarding these senior talents. The CEO turnover rate has increased substantially, and since more than two out of every three new CEOs reshuffle their management teams within the first two years, transitions cascade through the senior ranks. Two-thirds of executives report their organization is experiencing "some or many more" transitions than they did in the previous year (Keller and Meaney 2018).

Typically, organizations work extremely hard to identify and hire new executive talent—but then seem to rely on hope when it comes to making their investment successful.

Russell Reynolds Associates, one of the top ten search firms in the world, suggests 90 percent of the total cost of hiring a new executive is spent on the front end (Dineen 2021). This includes the recruitment and selection process such as search firm fees, assessment fees, cost of internal and external interviews, etc. As a result, only around 10 percent of the total executive hiring cost is spent on the back-end process such as a structured onboarding, executive transition coaching support, etc. This is a clear imbalance of the organizational investment.

When was the last time you experienced an accelerated and structured executive onboarding that was accompanied by a specialized executive transition coach?

A recent study found that 70 percent of CEOs are either underwhelmed by their onboarding process or have had no structured onboarding process at all (Byford, Watkins, and Triantogiannis 2017). This is quite a surprise as the bestselling book by Michael D. Watkins, *The First 90 Days*, has sold over a million copies and has been translated into twenty-four languages (International Institute for Management Development 2021). It was widely praised when it launched and was called the "Bible of onboarding." Revolutionary at the time, it provided a systematic onboarding process for new leaders that included a roadmap and an action plan for the first ninety days in a new role. However, it was written for a general audience with the subtitle *Critical Success Strategies for New Leaders at All Levels*— speaking to line managers, C-suite executives, entrepreneurs, and Human Resources leaders at the same time (Watkins 2003). Since then, there have been numerous books that touch upon the same topic using different angles. A selection of these are:

- *Right from the Start: Taking Charge in a New Leadership Role* (Ciampa and Watkins 1999)
- *The New Leader's 100-Day Action Plan: How to Take Charge, Build or Merge Your Team, and Get Immediate Results* (Bradt, Check, and Pedraza 2006)
- *Your Next Move: The Leader's Guide to Navigating Major Career Transitions* (Watkins 2009)
- *Your First 100 Days: Make Maximum Impact in Your New Role* (O'Keeffe 2011)
- *Before Onboarding: How to Integrate New Leaders for Quick and Sustained Results* (Burroughs 2011)
- *First-Time Leader: Foundational Tools for Inspiring and Enabling Your New Team* (Bradt and Davis 2014)
- *Transitions at the Top: What Organizations Must Do to Make Sure New Leaders Succeed* (Ciampa and Dotlich 2015)
- *Master Your Next Move: Proven Strategies for Navigating the First 90 Days* (Watkins 2019)

Yet, here we are, over two decades later, and many large and established organizations haven't managed to set up a structured onboarding process for their executive leaders. I recall several instances where my onboarding experience was rather underwhelming. In one instance, I was chased to complete the legally required compliance training although I had completed it. Mind you, nobody was chasing me to plan a series of meetings with key stakeholders to better understand the business and people challenges. Nobody was giving me a briefing about the team I had just inherited or setting up structured meetings to help me understand the leadership and culture of that organization as a newly on-boarded executive.

I must admit the executive onboarding experience tends to be somewhat neglected in a number of organizations, and I am puzzled as to why that is the case. Readers of this book will learn the multiple benefits that will arise from getting executive transitions right.

WHY ME

Over the last twenty-five years, I have gained a great deal of expertise going through executive transitions myself, having lived and successfully worked in five countries across six companies and sectors as an executive leader.

My professional background includes two decades of HR experience in some of the world's most admired organizations at the country, regional, and global leadership level, in both emerging and developed markets. I have seen firsthand why executives fail during their transitions and what are successful interventions.

In addition to the above, I have helped numerous executives successfully transition into new roles by maximizing their leadership impact, building high performing teams, and creating admired organizations as an executive transition coach. An executive transition coach combines the skills of an onboarding expert (aka a *First 90 Days* Transition Acceleration Adviser) coupled with elements of a leadership development coach. We combine the best of both worlds. It is common a transitioning executive will face many challenges that requires both a structured and more near term focus with elements that are tackled ideally for the mid and long term, too.

One client of mine described my rare combination of relevant experiences and our working together as "the triple-lens approach;" hence, combining the embodied experience and viewpoints of an HR leader, a transition coach, and a corporate executive.

EXISTING BODY OF WORK

Research conducted by Michael D. Watkins and Genesis has proven that the risk of executive transition failure can be reduced by 50 percent and the time for the newly on-boarded executive to break even by another 50 percent (Byford, Watkins, and Triantogiannis 2017). These are substantial gains made in a management world where executives are sometimes chasing Six Sigma type improvements (in other words, 3.4 defects per one million chances), such as improving the operating profit margin by 0.5 percent or increasing market share by 1 percent, reducing employment cost by 2–3 percent, etc. It surprises me to see how organizations are prepared to invest a lot of effort and attention in pursuing small, marginal gains, and it's even more surprising they are not focusing more on supporting executive transitions.

As highlighted above, there are a number of books available seeking to provide guidance and advice to transitioning executives. Most of these books are really useful and provide meaningful frameworks to the transitioning executive. However, the main issue with guided books is, essentially, it's all left up to the new executive to do it. The other problem perceived could be the lack of the so-called onboarding guru's actual experience of executive transitions. This book is grounded in my own embodied experience as an executive who has professionally and personally transitioned several times. In addition, there is a digital companion, e-learning, and one-on-one work available that are deemed to help the executive leader to put this body of work into practice.

WHO IS THIS FOR

This book has been written with a key readership in mind: senior leaders and executives who are embarking on their transition journey. That said, senior Human Resources leaders and coaches who have specialized in executive transitions will most certainly gain value from this work too.

WHY READ IT

This book provides an insider guide to executive transitions through a "triple-lens approach." As an executive going through a transition, you will be able to:

1. Understand why executive transitions feel more like being on a perpetual rollercoaster ride than a managerial process.
2. Identify the most common types of executive transition challenges and how to successfully maneuver them.
3. Avoid the ten biggest mistakes made during executive transitions.

4. Learn about the true cost of failed executive transitions.

5. Learn what support is out there to help with executive transitions.

6. Understand the business case behind successful executive transitions.

7. Learn proven interventions to transition more successfully into a new executive role.

8. Learn more about the "Dark Side" of executive transitions and how to best prepare for your last ninety days to leave behind a leadership legacy that far extends beyond your actual tenure.

A BRIEF SUMMARY OF THIS BOOK

The first part of the book looks at the **Foundations** of executive transitions. Where did it all begin, why onboarding frameworks can be useful, why care about the topic right now, and what the true definition of an executive transition coach is?

The second part of the book explores **Challenges & Failures.** We will look at existing organizational onboarding frameworks, what gets in the way, and what is the true cost of failed executive transitions. We will conclude this part with common executive transition challenges.

In the third part of the book, we will look at how executives can move **Toward Transition Mastery.** First, by looking at why getting executive transitions right makes a compelling business case before exploring key interventions to make executive transitions more successful. In the last two chapters of this part, I will introduce you to the Double Diamond Framework© of Executive Transitions.

The fourth and last part of the book looks at **Your Last 90 Days** and how executives can successfully transition out of a role.

CHAPTER 1

HISTORY OF EXECUTIVE TRANSITIONS

THE BEGINNING

It was a Friday in September, and I was working in my home office on a Zoom call with an executive transition coaching client. It was a so called "closure session" with one of the executives who had worked with me for the past twelve months on their executive transition into the C-suite.

The closure session is a chance for both the coach and the client to openly acknowledge what happened during the coaching program, to appreciate one another's work, to capture what was learned, and to officially end the coaching engagement.

This step is vital in leaving the client independent of the coach, self-correcting, and self-generating. Some of the questions touch upon what it was like for the client to have been part of the coaching program, what they learned, what the coach should change, emphasize, more or less, what the client appreciated the most and the least, and if there is anything else that needs to be shared with the coach.

We were reflecting on the past twelve months, and the client was acknowledging our work in a positive way and highlighting how much this intervention had helped them transition successfully, being able to reflect, and had increased their impact while being able to do this with ease and grace.

The client mentioned to me there was a feeling it had been a unique way of working with a coach and it was difficult to imagine initially how our working together would unfold when they signed up to work with me.

I thanked the client and said rather jokingly, "You are right, I have done a ton of research, and I've been coaching executives on their transition for a long time...I could probably write a book about it."

"Why not? I think you should," the client responded. I still get goosebumps when I reflect on that particular moment in time. It hit me hard, and then I froze when I saw the light in my client's eyes and the seriousness about the statement they had just made.

Personally, I never thought of shaping my embodied experience into a book, so it was eye-opening for me to suddenly realize the potential value in writing all of this up, to make an actual book out of it.

GETTING STARTED

The first action I took was to send a note to Anton Fishman, one of my contacts. Anton has had a long and successful career as an HR leader and partner at various organization consulting firms. One of the things I remembered was when he told me about the interim management practice and the work they had done to study the most successful interim managers. We met at a café in London, and Anton shared with me some of his previous experience. One of the early and formative stories he shared with me was about a speed networking exercise at a CIPD event back in 1987:

About the third or fourth conversation I had, this woman said, "Let me introduce myself. My name is Maria. I'm an interim HR director," and I said, I don't really know what that is. She said, "Let me tell you what I do on my first day when I start an assignment." This was in two or three minutes, and she started to go through how she entered a new assignment, what she was thinking about, who she was speaking to, why she was doing what she was doing, and how she was preparing herself for the next six months before she left.

It was a revelation for me because out of her mouth was coming the essence of what we had already been building into our transition coaching. That revelation was a sudden appreciation that here was someone whose job was to transition, deliver, and exit as a profession. This is what she did, and she was proficient at it. Somehow she'd figured out how to do it because here she was telling me how she did it. I left there with a real insight into the possibility there was a population of people like her, and somehow embedded in this was a collective knowledge and insight into how to manage these transitions effectively. Because if they didn't, they would fail in their assignments."

SHOCKINGLY HIGH FAILURE RATE

Research suggests between 30–50 percent of all executive transitions fail during the first eighteen to twenty-four months (Masters 2009; Keller and Meaney 2018). The cost of replacing an executive can be anywhere between ten to thirty times their salary (Fatemi 2016). Not to mention, the executive will have to find a new role after a failed transition. If the career break is severe enough, they may never land another executive role again. Or their career trajectory may be negatively impacted as a result.

Given the high stakes, I found it very surprising how little good guidance is available to new executives about how to transition more effectively and efficiently into a new leadership role. This is particularly true during a global pandemic! There are many reasons for this shockingly high failure rate.

Lots of my fellow executive coaches, HR leaders, and I have been focused on rethinking the way we support executives during their transition as well as how to do this most effectively in a virtual environment. Personally, I have been on a mission and have spent hundreds of hours since 2014 trying to answer one critical question.

THE MILLION-DOLLAR QUESTION

How can executives successfully transition, avoiding the biggest mistakes, and do it with ease and grace—and how do they do this when working remotely?

I have had my fair share of executive transition mishaps and sometimes failures. In particular, I have found my executive transition mistakes—and sometimes those of my executive transition clients—to be most helpful when it comes to learning and adapting before moving forward.

Before we get to the second chapter of this book, I'd like to share a few personal thoughts.

When going through executive transitions as a leader, I wasted *so* much time with trial and error. I have seen executive coaching clients doing the same, often before reaching out to work with me—and that's true for so many of us.

We have talents and experiences we would love to share with the world. We want to play on a bigger stage and have an even larger impact. That's the goal, but getting there is often quite a challenge. We often feel like we have to figure it out on our own. Or we'd be open to learning from others but just aren't sure who to turn to, where to look, or where to start.

How confident am I that I knew exactly where to invest, and how to prioritize my executive capabilities to transitions most successfully into a new role? It can feel overwhelming at times. I certainly felt that way often.

While I have been training and practicing as a coach for over a decade, in 2014 I started specializing in helping leaders going through executive transitions.

I wish I had access to this body of work and one-on-one support when I went through my first transition back in 2005 because I made so many mistakes that wasted time and energy that could have been avoided. Given I was hired as a top talent, the organization assumed I knew enough to succeed. The resources made available to me internally were nowhere near sufficient for a proper leadership transition, however. So why reinvent the wheel when you can save yourself time and effort and get to the effective transition insights—that much faster?

DEFINING EXECUTIVE TRANSITIONS

How do we define an executive transition? What is the definition of a successful executive transition? Rather than delivering my own, I'd like to cite two existing definitions from McKinsey & Co.:

> We define a transition as the period (which can last up to 18 months) after an executive has assumed his or her new C-level responsibilities. And we define "successful transitions" as those where executives say they aligned and mobilized their organizations very or extremely well around their initial objectives during transition and have met their overall objectives very or extremely well during their tenure (Chandran 2015).

Anton Fishman, one of the early thought leaders in this space described their process of executive transition coaching as:

...there are specific coaching interventions for executive transitions that can enable people to become effective through insight, guidance, and support. Structured transition coaching provides executives with insight into the actions and practices best avoided, it makes visible the traps potentially waiting for them, and helps them rapidly amplify positive actions and insights.

Our experience as coaches of bright and insightful senior and experienced people in transition is this more directive guidance early on in their transition is appreciated, valued and actioned. The guidance being seen as immediately relevant and when highlighted often self-evident, leading to early and effective application with almost immediate gratification with very short cycle action and reward. In my experience this is the only coaching context in which this more directive or pedagogic style works well and even here it should give way to classic coaching disciplines after the first few weeks.

Over the last twenty years, I have not only read but also applied most of what has been considered best practice in executive transitions. This includes *The First 90 Days* framework published over eighteen years ago by Michael Watkins, as well as some of the more recent work published (Watkins 2003). In the end, I have come to take the very best elements of each model and publicized research to create my own Double Diamond Framework© of Executive Transitions, which

I'll describe in Chapters 12 and 13. I would like to assure the readers of this book everything that follows from here on is grounded in research as well as in what actually works in the organizational practice of executive transitions.

In the next chapter, I'll describe some of the existing models of onboarding and the science and intentionality behind them.

CHAPTER 2

THE SCIENCE & INTENTIONALITY OF ONBOARDING FRAMEWORKS

Do you enjoy roller-coaster rides? Whether you enjoy them or not, I will demonstrate why executive transitions often feel like a roller-coaster ride.

In this chapter, I'm going to focus on the science and intentionality of onboarding frameworks—their strengths but also weaknesses. Together, we are going to see why "figuring it out" isn't sufficient.

In the previous chapter, I used the analogy of a roller coaster when referring to executive transitions. Let's explore this topic a little more in-depth. You may by now be asking the question what executive transitions have in common with amusement parks.

THE MAGNITUDE OF CHANGE IMPACTING TRANSITIONS

First off: Some numbers are simply undeniable when you think about them. About one third of the leaders in an organization undergo a transition any given year. I have observed this myself over the years. As Michael D. Watkins put it in one of the *Harvard Business Review* interviews with Jeff Kehoe, "Today, people almost have a career of transitions rather than a few transitions in their career."

At the same time, the pace and complexity of transitions are increasing. Many executives are being pushed further and faster, organizations are taking bigger bets on talent, and as a result, executives have to undergo more tricky transitions.

As we can see the pace and magnitude of change are constantly rising in the business world, so it is no surprise that executive transitions are increasingly common: CEO turnover rate has increased by almost 80 percent, with 32 percent being forced out of their role. This has gone up from 9.8 percent in 2003 to 17.5 percent in 2018 (Birshan, Meakin, and Strovink 2016). Since 69 percent of new CEOs reshuffle their management teams within the first two years, transitions cascade through the senior ranks. The 67 percent of leaders reported their organizations now experience "some or many more" transitions than they did in the previous year (Birshan, Meakin, and Strovink 2016; Keller and Meaney 2018).

Furthermore, studies from Genesis Advisers demonstrate each executive transition directly effects on average a minimum of twelve leaders in the same organization (Caspar and Halbye 2011).

Is the image of a roller coaster becoming clearer now?

Now, let's add the following.

THE EXCITEMENT OF THE NEW EXECUTIVE ROLE VS. THE REALITY

Executives who are going through their transition initially come across their first positive interactions with various stakeholders. This often results in initial euphoria and a sense of real excitement. Then...they are often faced with complex situations. They become more aware of substantial challenges, but undeniably, there are also opportunities to note.

When executives move into their first set of actions, they experience their first setbacks or rejection. Or worse, they come across what can be called a "deafening silence." When digging deeper into organizational issues, they may face multiple and sometimes overlapping types of transitions that are often ambiguous in nature.

Think of the scientist who was the best R&D leader in a country R&D unit who is now being asked to step up to become the managing director of the R&D Center for the entire region, managed out of the corporate HQ. A natural career progression, some might think, but the executive transition coach and the leader know this includes many of the following challenges: the big promotion challenge, the leading former peers (fellow country R&D leaders) challenge, the corporate diplomacy challenge, the international move challenge, and the cross-functional challenge (Watkins 2019).

These are already five of the top challenges in executive transitions! Depending on the circumstances and mandate, there may also be other challenges ahead such as a re-alignment challenge of one or more R&D centers, (Watkins 2019).

Furthermore, what often follows after a promotion or an external hire is a rather vague mandate. The executive in transition often finds out after their appointment the main goals and priorities of key stakeholders may not align very well, or even worse, they are contradictory. As soon as the incoming executive observes major interpretations of their mandate, the best approach would be to share their observations in a non-judgmental way with their hiring manager and try to re-align or re-negotiate the mandate accordingly.

As if this wasn't enough, another challenge may prove to be the inherited leadership team. The executive in transition needs to quickly find out about the team members' capabilities, behaviors, motivation, and mindset. Who, in that team of direct reports, is a genuine support to the new leader? Who may not be? How to go about finding that out?

One executive transition client of mine once told me she had inquired information about the leadership team, such as their background and performance and potential ratings through the HR function. The prevailing opinion and data made available to her by the HR leader suggested she had inherited a high performing team with real high potentials in the mix. So, when we were reflecting on the data and feedback that the leader had received, the following questions emerged that needed further exploration with HR and the leader's line manager, who was a member of the Executive Committee:

- If the majority of the team is frequently performing at a high level, with some of them being high potentials, then how come that the leader's predecessor was let go?
- If the previous executive leader was definitely not a top performer and ultimately left for performance or behavior reasons, how much can the new leader trust their judgment including the assessment and ratings that were given to the team members by that same leader?
- And for what reason was nobody from within the team considered for the top role?

Well, the leader found out after two frank conversations with the HR leader and line manager that some of the team members' performance assessments and potential ratings may not have been objectively granted. On a side note, they found out that one of the newly inherited team members had gone through the hiring process for the top job but was unsuccessful. After my client had joined the organization, that same individual happened to be quite disruptive during leadership team meetings, and on more than one occasion they tried to undermine the incoming executive.

The executive leader in transition utilized me as an external coach to assess the inherited leadership team. They underwent a leadership team intervention that included a new leader assimilation, agreed, and set up clear team ground rules, and only a few months into the role they performed a partial refresh of the leadership team.

It's not always negative. Let me share an early in career example of mine. I had to deal with situations that were quite multifaceted, that contained significant challenges but also great opportunities. I got a very early promotion as one of the early in career employees in an entire region to step up to a Head of HR role. And at the same time, I did not own the skills and capabilities to be effective at that level and in that particular role. With the support of colleagues, key stakeholders, my (functional) line manager and an executive coach, I was able to bounce back and to perform in the new position and make a positive impact.

When conducting stakeholder interviews, there are likely to be more than one set of stakeholders to be engaged, entertained, and kept in the loop. They may pose potentially conflicting needs to the new executive. Stakeholders will typically include the executive's line manager, a subset of peers, a subset of direct reports, and any other internal or external person who has an influence on the success and outcomes of the role.

All of this results in high demand on the executive's energy and time, which in return can result in exhaustion and fatigue early on. Those who "survive" this kind of grueling experience can expect a recovery phase before they are dragged into a repeating cycle. Here again, the support of an executive transition coach can be immensely beneficial. The same can be said about having an influential and wise mentor, internally or externally.

There comes the roller coaster again!

POPULAR ONBOARDING FRAMEWORKS

We now know executive transitions are one of the most delicate undertakings for any executive and their organization. Arguably, there are some great guidebooks out there–whether it is the 2003 book from Michael Watkins called *The First 90 Days* (F90Days), or the 2006 book by Bradt, Check, and Pedraza titled *The New Leader's 100-Day Action Plan.*

Both books are useful and address a good part of a manager's onboarding. *The First 90 Days* uses a so-called STARS framework, looking at both challenges and opportunities in each phase) as outlined below (Watkins 2003):

Start-Up → Turnaround → Accelerated Growth →Realignment →Sustaining Success

The New Leader's 100-Day Action Plan (TNL100DAP) uses a somewhat similar framework. It is an eight-step model that is time-bound from before onboarding to day one hundred in a new role (Bradt, Check, and Pedraza 2006).

Step 1: **Position Yourself** for Success
Step 2: Leverage the **Fuzzy Front End**
Step 3: Take Control of **Day One (Day 1)**
Step 4: Co-create **Burning Imperative (Day 30)**
Step 5: Embed **Milestones (Day 45)**
Step 6: Jump-start **Early Wins (Day 60)**
Step 7: Complete Organization **Role Sort (Day 70)**
Step 8: **Evolve** Leadership, Practices, Culture **(Day 100)**

THE LIMITATION OF PURISTIC 90–120 DAY FRAMEWORKS

While some organizations try to help newly appointed executives by supplying them with mentors or informal "buddy" networks, less than half of external hires and not even a third of internal ones find these to be helpful (Wheeler 2008). Watkins came back to revisit his model from 2003, and in a 2017 *Harvard Business Review* (*HBR*) article co-authored with Byford and Triantogiannis, he suggested "Onboarding Isn't Enough."

While the above models have their merits, the key question is whether a 90–120 Day focus is enough to propel an executive into a new leadership role.

In a McKinsey & Co. study, 1,195 C-suite executives were surveyed and most of them considered an executive transition to last much longer than one hundred days—more likely four to eighteen months (Birshan, Meakin, and Strovink 2016).

SOME EXECUTIVES – EVEN THOSE WITH THE MOST SUCCESSFUL TRANSITIONS – NEED MORE THAN 100 DAYS TO ADAPT TO A NEW C-LEVEL ROLE

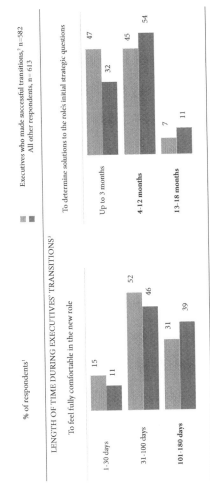

Figure 2.1. Most executives need more than one hundred days to adapt to a new C-level role. Reproduced with permission from McKinsey & Co. (Chandran, de la Boutetiere, and Dewar 2015).

THEORY VS. PRACTICE—THE CHRO CASE

Rudi Kindts, former CHRO of BAT who turned to coaching after retiring form a successful corporate career, said in our interview:

> I think what I saw myself (as an executive leader) and what I also see as a coach is the misconception that an executive transition is a single event. With a single event I mean that could also be the first ninety days.

> As Michael Watkins refers to, there are the ninety days, and I think that's not right. It's not the reality. The reality is transition is a process and not a single event, and somewhere for me, there are three phases in it.

> The first one is arrival, and that's where I think The First 90 Days is good because that's arriving or onboarding. The second phase I see is to transition. It's only later that I think brings the third stage of thriving.

> You can almost say it is going to be very difficult to thrive if you didn't arrive well, if you didn't survive, or if that didn't go too well. The first time I transitioned to the group HR director role with BAT, I was busy with the arrival, and I went through the first ninety days like in most cases. I made the framework my own because it isn't complete, and there is no mention of surviving.

> I only understood the surviving through the feedback I received from Paul, the group CEO. I thought to myself, Oh, hang on, I thought I had arrived! I didn't use that terminology, but I thought I was there. Oh, not. Right.

Oh, so that is a first learning I saw. Still, thinking of organizations, when the onboarding or the arrival event has been successful, people are transitioning. It is more likely you will almost philosophically transition your whole life because things change constantly.

So you could arrive in a certain situation, and while you're surviving, the situation has changed. You're surviving again. I mean, when are you ever going to thrive? Or you're arriving on this aspect, but you're surviving on another one, and you're thriving on another one. So, it's not linear. The whole thing is a circle. That was the first misconception of what transition is, in my experience.

What underpins surviving is being able to let go, particularly to let go of your comfort zone, and to embrace what is new when it is being expected. To be honest, you usually don't have any experience of it. So again, I got this through feedback and thought to myself, What is going on? I'm again going through that transition with Paul, the CEO. So somewhere, I had this mental image my transition or promotion to the group executive team had to do with representing the functional line to the executive team, and that was wrong.

JACK WELCH AND JEFF IMMELT ON *THE FIRST 90 DAYS*

The somewhat controversial ex-General Electric (GE) CEO and chairman Jeff Immelt made the following statement on January 7, 2005, four years into his tenure as a CEO during a so-called candid conversation:

*One of the things Jack said early on that I think is totally
right is it's a marathon. It's not a sprint. All these books
about the first ninety days are kind of rubbish in many
ways. You have to have a plan. You have to stick with
it. You have to modify it at times, but every day you've
got to get up and play hard (Byrne, 2005).*

From 2001 to 2017 and during Immelt's tenure as a CEO,
shares of GE dropped 30 percent, while the S&P 500 rose by
134 percent (Shen 2017). GE restated its earnings the same
year the above interview was given (2005) and agreed to pay
the SEC $50 million to settle allegations of accounting fraud
in 2009. Despite Immelt's dislike of structured onboarding
programs, he had an empty corporate jet following his
corporate jet in case there were delays with his primary jet
(Muoio 2017).

Well before the crisis, research had established transition-ac-
celeration coaching halves the time required for new executives to become fully effective in their roles. Given you,
your team, and your new leader's team are all dealing with
the stresses of responding to the crisis, executive transition
coaches can be impactful. They are particularly helpful when
they understand the organization, the company culture, and
the stakeholder environment. Work buddies and coaches
play complementary roles in advising new executives on the
challenges they face and providing a safe space within which
to discuss them.

PROVEN BENEFITS OF STRUCTURED TRANSITIONS

Genesis Advisers surveyed a sample of executives who received executive transition support, as well as their hiring managers, HR business partners, and the coaches providing the integration support (Watkins 2017b). To measure the impact of the executive transition support, they asked each group to estimate by what margin the time would be reduced for the executives to become fully effective. The results were definitive: the right support for integration can halve the time for new leaders to get up to speed. Not only that, the research suggests when supported by an executive transition coach, executives can also increase the likelihood of a successful transition by 50 percent (Wheeler 2009).

THE NEW LEADER'S 100-DAY ACTION PLAN (TNL100DAP)

George Bradt, one of the authors of TNL100DAP, recently blogged the "essence of the 700 articles" he has written for *Forbes* over the years (Bradt 2021). There, he summarizes his "most helpful ideas":

1. Converge, then evolve: The leader needs to grasp the context and become part of the team before helping team members to evolve. Timing is crucial here as moving too fast may result in organ rejection and moving too slowly may mean the leader fails to deliver what's expected of them. Bradt rightly points out the leader should conform to the organizational culture first instead of trying to change it until "they have earned that right."
2. Be an other-focused leader: Here, the suggestion is to be mindful of the fact not too many people care in particular

for the leader, but they care more about what the leader can do for them.

3. Own your own choices: Doing this would mean refusing to play the victim role. While doing this, the recommendation is for the leader to "do their best to support others that can solve them or solve it themselves."

4. Choose influence over direction: To inspire true commitment, the key is to work with principles (not policies or guidelines) and co-create to best enable leadership team members.

5. Be, Do, and Say with Integrity: As a leader, aligning actions with words and underlying beliefs is essential, especially because "everything communicates."

Bradt cross-references his BRAVE leadership framework above, working through:

Behaviors—What impact? (Implementation)
Relationships—How to connect?
Attitudes—How to win? (Choices)
Values—What matters and why? (Purpose)
Environment—Where to play? (Context)

BEFORE ONBOARDING

Some of the executive transition thought leaders have indicated a different but complementary perspective of onboarding. It is grounded in the suggestion to begin the onboarding process *before* starting in the new role. The 2011 seminal work of Michael K. Burroughs, *Before Onboarding: How to Integrate New Leaders for Quick and Sustained Results,* defines executive integration as a "facilitated process that prepares new senior leaders in advance of their start date to arrive fully briefed and equipped to get the right results quickly and avoid costly, preventable mistakes."

It goes beyond the concepts of F90Days and TNL100DAP. His work suggests the executive integration process:

- begins **before** the new executive's start date,
- is **overseen** by a process consultant (e.g., an executive coach who has specialized in executive transitions),
- **involves the new executive leader's universe**, so line manager, peers and direct reports (at a minimum), and
- extends beyond the start date for **at least the first ninety days** (Burroughs 2021).

Burroughs goes further to recommend, "Executive Coaching has proved to be the most effective developmental vehicle for executives." He also rightly claims an experienced executive transition coach is more appropriate than a leadership development coach (Burroughs 2021).

Burrough's new leader integration process consists of six stages. These are entry, interview, documentation, debriefing, kick-off meeting, and lastly, follow-up. The book is further enriched with interview questions that can be used with various stakeholders. These are the onboarding executive's line manager, peers (if there are any), direct reports, key customers, major suppliers, group leaders, trustees, major donors, and others. The executive transition coach will play a part in each of these six stages (Burroughs 2021).

The last framework I'd like to share with you has been developed by Genesis Advisers and Egon Zehnder. This framework serves as a guide for organizations to develop the onboarding of executives through the stages of maturity (Triantogiannis 2017):

1. Basic Orientation → 2. Active Assimilation → 3. Accelerated Integration

To do this, five core transition tasks are required from the executive (Triantogiannis 2017):

- Diagnose the Business Context
- Take Charge of the Team
- Align with Stakeholders
- Understand & Embrace the Culture
- Shape Strategic Direction

Given the many research studies that have focused on senior leadership onboarding and executive integration and transitions, it is undeniable there is a proven, scientifically measured benefit for both the executive and their organization to make it their primary interest to do this effectively and successfully. The most obvious reason is to reduce the executive transition risk by 50 percent or more and reducing the time to break-even by another 50 percent through an accelerated integration (Wheeler 2008).

COMMON BUILDING BLOCKS

By now, we have reviewed what are arguably the best existing onboarding frameworks in the world. Reflecting on the information above and bearing in mind many other onboarding models and frameworks I have studied, implemented, and tested during the course of the last two decades, there are some over-arching stepping stones and phases that emerge.

I have learned the best in the world do the following things differently, which ensures the greatest chance of success when it comes to transitioning executives:

1. Apply a **structured and yet fluid framework** that allows for **convergence and divergence** at different times during executive transitions.
2. Support the executive with a **specialized executive transition coach** (ideally externally engaged).
3. Focus the executive's attention and energy on all **critical stakeholder groups** but pay **particular attention to their line manager and direct reports** since these are most supportive of the executive's onboarding process (Watkins 2017a).

Given the above insights, I've developed a unique framework I'm very excited to share with you: the **Double Diamond Framework© of Executive Transitions**. It will be covered in detail in Chapters 12 and 13. In the next chapter, I will be focusing on why mastering executive transitions matters now more than ever before.

CHAPTER 3

WHY NOW?

In August 2021, there was a buzz word that was making headlines, namely that of "The Great Resignation" (Kane and Ocean 2021).

I remember once I met our newly appointed CHRO who had joined our company from another organization, and this visit was part of his onboarding process which had been meticulously organized. He concluded our conversation with a short glimpse of his onboarding plan. It was strategically structured and appropriately supported.

Let's face it: All executives should have a meticulous onboarding process that is well organized and supported by a transition coach. Not all of us may have that luxury; however, this is where the onboarding books come in. You've read *The First 90 Days* or another onboarding book and you're still puzzled as to where to start, what to do, and how to do it? Well, that is exactly how I have often felt throughout my executive career (Watkins 2003).

I felt compelled to write this book, not only because of my own experiences throughout my career, but also because there are way too many executives failing during their transition. The failure rate is around the 40 percent mark (Keller and Meaney 2018). This rate of failure is coupled with an increasingly reduced tenure of senior leaders in role and organizations struggling to win the war for talent at the same time. To me, this issue seems like a huge bubble that is going to burst in the foreseeable future. When it does, the execution of corporate strategies may be seriously at risk, with a negative impact on the financials of the business.

What further motivated me to write this book is the fact most of the thought leaders in the executive transition space are either pure academics or happen to be consultants working for large consulting firms and ultimately keen to market their products and solutions. Thus far, I haven't come across a practitioner who has written about this topic, combining the latest research with grounded leadership and organization practices that work in the real world of work in the form of a book.

This book explores the intersection of executive leaders and their career transitions, reflecting on the available research (theory) of transitions and the reality of it (practice) and how this process can be supported by the organization.

Michael K. Burroughs, a thought leader in the executive onboarding space, told me in our interview, "One of the problems that I have with *The First 90 Days* is it's all left up to the new executive to do it" (Watkins 2003). This may be the reason why smart executives seek external support to make their transition most successful.

We will now find out why executives are exponentially challenged with an increased risk of failure.

ATTRITION

If we assume a rather conservative 10 percent attrition rate per year, we're looking at somewhere between 300,000 to 450,000 executive transitions in the US per year. If we then apply the 40 percent failure rate, the issue becomes truly magnified, but we shouldn't stop here. In the US alone, the average number of jobs in a lifetime is twelve, according to a 2019 longitudinal study by the Bureau of Labor Statistics of the so-called baby boomer generation (Chappell 2013; Association of Executive Search and Leadership Consultants 2013). This demonstrates the number of times leaders will transition throughout their professional lifespan.

Jeff Warren, a managing director of Russell Reynolds Associates, shared data around the percentage of portfolio company CEOs that are turned over during the investment lifecycle:

In actuality, it's 73 percent. So nearly three out of four investments undergo a CEO transition during the investment lifecycle. It's a pretty staggering statistic if we think about it. If we go one step further, and we've taken a look at this, almost 60 percent of CEO transitions happened within the first two years. Now, while some of this is probably necessary, the number is far too high, and indicates a much bigger challenge (Warren 2021).

In 2019, a staggering 28.7 million people were employed by the Fortune 500 alone, currently representing about two thirds of the US economy with $13.7 trillion in revenue (Fortune 2021). The total number of people working in the US currently stands at 160 million people (Bureau of Labor Statistics 2021). If we apply a simple formula assuming about 2–3 percent of that population are executives, we're looking at roughly 3 to 4.8 million executives in the US alone.

OPPORTUNISTIC LEADERS

The Executive Mobility Report found 67 percent of the executives surveyed are likely to consider a new opportunity immediately (Association of Executive Search and Leadership Consultants 2013; Chappell 2013). Another 48.9 percent reported they were actively looking for a new role. Only 5.3 percent of executives worldwide did not consider making a job change when the survey was conducted.

From a risk management point of view, organizations must ensure they have solid succession plans in place and are prepared to replace and onboard new executives now and even more so in the future.

ESCAPING LEADERS

According to a 2021 comprehensive global study conducted by Microsoft titled the "Work Trend Index Annual Report," 41 percent of employees are considering leaving their current employer and 46 percent say they are planning to move jobs because they can now work remotely (Anders et al. 2021).

Two of the seven urgent trends the study has identified are "Leaders are out of touch with employees and need a wake-up call" and "Authenticity will spur productivity and well-being" (Anders et al. 2021). Both of these are topics that will be dealt with later in this book when we look at typical executive transition challenges as well as successful interventions for executive transitions.

INCREASED SPAN OF CONTROL

It gets better: Harvard Business School research into C-level roles over the past two decades found that the CEO's average span of control, measured by the number of direct reports, has doubled, rising from about five in the mid-1980s to almost ten in the mid-2000s (Neilson and Wulf 2021). The jump in the chief executive's area of responsibility is probably also due to the fact organizations are more complex, more globally dispersed, and more strictly scrutinized than those of previous generations. This in return means more C-suite leaders who ultimately will transition at some point throughout their career, multiple times over.

INCREASED DEMANDS FROM CEOS

A study conducted by Boston Consulting Group found the number of performance requirements for a newly appointed CEO has increased six-fold between 1995 and 2013 (Morieux 2011). Back in 1995, CEOs were typically measured against four to seven main KPIs, and against twenty-five to forty in 2013. At the same time, the level of organizational complexity increased by a factor of thirty-five (Morieux 2011).

If we applied a linear regression to the CEO tenure trend (that well extends into other C-suite leaders), then the real magnitude of this issue becomes apparent. Imagine for a moment the economic impact on the entire world. In addition to this challenge, the research also hints at a drop of employee engagement levels by as much as 14 percent. Coupled with lower job satisfaction from 60 percent to 43 percent, the modern-day CEO will not only be in charge of a far more skeptical and dispirited workforce but will also need to work much harder to secure its backing. When we add the higher levels of scrutiny by various stakeholder groups, including the media, it becomes clear why it gets very lonely pretty quickly high up in the corner office (Torres and Tollman 2013).

SIGNIFICANT COST

CEOs in the US who depart after eighteen months on the job cost small-cap companies an estimated $12 million each (Ciampa and Dotlich 2015). For large-cap companies, the figure is $52 million per CEO. Some research estimates these departures add up to a minimum loss in the United States of $14 billion each year. Other research shows a failed leader transition can cost 2.5 to 20 times the executive's yearly compensation (Nawaz 2017; Paese 2021).

Jeff Warren also shared some data points around the cost associated with portfolio companies CEOs' attrition that sits at 73 percent during the investment lifecycle recently:

> Let's turn now to what the financial costs of that turnover could be. So, there are indirect (costs) as well as

direct (costs). There are a number of opportunity costs that can inflate the total cost to dramatic numbers here, oftentimes twenty times the compensation that's actually paid (Warren 2021).

Richard Thackray, managing director at Partners Group, further emphasized during the same call:

I think we've all been in situations where a CEO change connotes a lack of performance in a business, and that's going to extend months, maybe years. If we get it wrong, I think you could make an argument in a nice middle-sized company with, say, $50 million of EBITDA you lose a year.

You know, that then becomes really material. You've lost, let's say you're looking for 10 percent growth, that's five million in lost EBITDA even in the following year. It flows all the way through to the end of the investment. So that could be $60 million at the back end if it's a twelve-time multiple, and it's $5 million in free cash flow that could go to paying down debt or reinvesting in the company. So, the numbers scale very big, very quickly into really sizable impact. If you think about it, particularly on the soft cost side (Thackray 2021).

Jeff Warren continues:

We also have damage to the client base and brand reputation. There it hits employee morale when leaders are changed. There are oftentimes other changes that happen on the management team that just kills the momentum. So, the costs here are real and measurable (Warren 2021).

SHORTAGE OF TALENT

Given the current shortage of talent, coupled with a declining workforce in the developed economies (China just reported its first-ever population decline in forty years), this will further amplify the issue (Sun 2021). Let's face it, this trend has been ongoing for years. As the leading talent management consultant Josh Bersin puts it, "Much of the top talent you need might already be in your company, but where are they and how do you transition them to a new role?" (Bersin 2021)

All of the above would suggest executive transitions should have the highest priority in organizations and receive appropriate attention and investment.

VERTICAL VS. HORIZONTAL DEVELOPMENT

The definition of horizontal development is pretty straightforward. This is all about acquiring more knowledge, skills, and information. Vertical development, however, is an entirely different ball game. The Center for Creative Leadership (CCL) has a good definition for it: "It's about more complex and sophisticated ways of thinking. It's called vertical development because it's based on levels, or stages, of thinking. It involves gaining new perspectives and leadership mindsets needed to make your business strategy work" (Leading Effectively Staff 2020). An example could be when executives learn to tackle a challenge through inquiry—questions, observation, and reflection—before jumping into advocating, lobbying, or deciding. This way of leadership can open the door to deeper understanding, greater clarity, more options, and multiple right answers—which are particularly needed for leading in complex, uncertain situations.

Rudi Kindts, ex-CHRO of BAT and executive coach, spoke about vertical development in our interview. He combines the rare combination of having been a corporate executive who made it to the highest level in a large organization coupled with being a professional coach:

But there is a necessity to transition personally. That's where personal development comes in, I can see it now as a coach, and it was true for myself as well. At the beginning of our careers, the expectations are that we are an expert and we can deliver.

So we go from expert and then we transition to being an achiever, that means we start to manage others. So, we output results. Right? Now we're going to drive results. But the higher we come in an organization, assuming we talk about vertical transitions, we also have horizontal transitions. When you look at them vertically, when you are in a certain position, it's not about your expertise. It's even not about striving for results. Do you really strive for results and drive for results? That's a given.

Now, your personal transition is how you make meaning, and I think once I made that transition at that high level, you need to be able to think longer term instead of the shorter term. You need to be able to hold different perspectives to not knowing and then finally come to a view and a perspective on all those things. So, it's a true vertical transition. Is that a transition that an executive leader will purposefully and deliberately be going to take? That's where I think executive transition coaching comes in.

Because when you make the transition, what do you value? How does that change? How do you allocate your time, etc.? That second one is as an individual. If you make a leadership transition at the level I made that transition, I was too much in the beginning, in the arrival, too much on the achieving and experience. I had to change based on feedback from our Group CEO.

Based on the above, it is evident 2020 has changed the world of work forever and the future of work will become more complex both for transitioning executives and organizations in equal measure. Because of the shortage of talent, attrition, and increased demands from CEOs, there is a need for this process to be of utmost strategic priority. We will look at what support is available to transitioning executives and how organizations are supporting them in the following chapters.

In the next chapter, I will outline the main differences between leadership development coaches and transition advisers.

CHAPTER 4

THE DIFFERENCE BETWEEN TRANSITION ADVISERS & LEADERSHIP DEVELOPMENT COACHES

___

For the sake of simplicity, I am going to grossly over-simplify the topic of coaching in this chapter. Many coaches will likely disagree with me and argue the role of a coach is indeed very different. That being said, I am inviting you to bear with me as I highlight the main differences between a transition adviser and a leadership development coach, before outlining what an executive transition coach does.

LEADERSHIP DEVELOPMENT COACHES

As an executive, you may have heard of, or worked with, a leadership development coach. The approach can sometimes be more backward-looking, often reactive with the coaching occurring after a problem has been identified or behavior has been flagged to change or improve.

The view for a leadership development coach is often to work with the leader, their line manager, and sometimes Human Resources to assess existing competencies, behaviors, and leadership styles. While their remit can vary quite a bit, most of them are focusing on self-awareness and leadership (behavior) changes. According to the education and training of the coach, their methodologies and frameworks can vary widely.

The strategy is often to identify any competency and behavior gaps and propose mitigation strategies. The achieved results then flow into the executive's development plan. The skills a leadership development coach requires are often rooted in deep behavioral insights and the typical duration of support is over an extended period, quite commonly over a twelve- to eighteen-month time period (Keller and Meaney 2018).

Sometimes after a period in the new role, whether there was a good onboarding process or not, a behavior or competency gets flagged as needing work, e.g., there could be a narrow coaching remit. Sometimes this remit is correctly diagnosed, other times the behavior is merely the tip of the iceberg of things that are not working out in the new role. As a result, leadership development coaching several months into an executive role could trigger bigger issues to work on.

TRANSITION ADVISERS

A transition adviser, however, provides a very different kind of support. Their approach is rather proactive and forward-looking to "address common traps before they occur" (Watkins 2017).

The view for a transition adviser is to "assess the business situation and the executive's approach to their new role." Hence the focus is clearly on "transition and action planning." The applied methodology is very structured, and frameworks are applied to support the executive (Watkins 2017).

The strategy is to help the executive to create a plan and build momentum and manage themselves in the new executive role. The concrete results are a clearly defined ninety to one hundred-day action plan. The skills a transition adviser needs are more on the business acumen side and the duration is usually time-bound and varies between three to nine months (Watkins 2017).

EXECUTIVE TRANSITION COACHES

Executive transition coaches (such as I) combine the best of both roles. Some aspects of accelerating the executive's transition will lie in a structured onboarding framework, whereas other aspects are to be found in the leadership development and behavioral space. In addition to that, certain activities don't fall into either of these two buckets.

Let me share a concrete case study of a C-suite client who worked with me on their executive transition. In this example, I will bring together the elements I mentioned above. To maintain client confidentiality and the integrity of my practice, I won't be providing more details about the client. What I can reveal is initially she and I contracted individually, and as soon as she started in her role, her organization supported the executive transition coaching financially. For ease of reference, let's just call her Natalie. Natalie was tasked to head up an international matrixed organization with more than 200,000 FTE. Below is an outline of the steps that were taken as well as some of the high-level results that were achieved.

This was a twelve-month executive transition coaching engagement. We had met briefly when I was delivering a masterclass at an HR conference a few weeks before our engagement. The executive had asked for my business card and had hinted to me that a transition lay ahead.

A few weeks later we got in touch via email and Natalie told me the chairman of the firm had asked her to "get packing" as the global C-suite promotion was about to happen. Before that, there had been a grueling hiring process that had taken several weeks, including many key stakeholder interviews, the involvement of several key executives, board members, the chairman, and an external search firm.

We set up a coaching chemistry call. At times it is overlooked that choosing an executive coach is a highly personal matter. The executive is seeking support to improve one of the most important aspects of their life, namely their career. On the back end of our call, we were happy to go ahead and agreed to things verbally during a brief telephone conversation.

The fact I received a call from Natalie roughly two months before starting in the new role to kick off the executive transition coaching engagement was crucial for many reasons. It is important to start the executive transition coaching engagement ideally *before* starting in the new role. "New leader integration" or "pre-boarding" occurs for the most part *before* the start date, not after (Burroughs 2011). "Pre-boarding" will give the executive leader valuable time they most likely won't have when they have started in their new position. It also helps to establish a baseline, and in some cases, even allows for first relationships to be built. While popular management literature suggests the first ninety to one hundred days are crucial for the executive's success, we should all know by now the ninety, sixty, or even thirty days leading up to day one are equally important (Watkins 2003; Bradt 2009).

CXO CASE STUDY

As soon as we had agreed on working together, we got started. This particular executive transition coaching involved several significant challenges. These included a big promotion, the corporate diplomacy challenge, and an international move challenge. Furthermore, a turnaround challenge, a cross-functional challenge, and a realignment challenge—since the previous C-suite incumbent had been let go prematurely. Given all of this, the credibility of the function and its focus had to be re-established as well as managing a business portfolio challenge and, lastly, a cross-functional move challenge.

CXO CLIENT'S CHALLENGE

Figure 4.1. Image Source: This image is self-created (the eight transition types are from the 2019 book *Master Your Next Move* by Michael Watkins).

From an executive transition coaching point of view, working with a specialized coach is always recommended as soon as the executive is facing more than one challenge. As you can see this particular case included seven main challenges and many more intricacies on top. There was no planned succession, and a few months into our coaching a CEO was hired who became Natalie's new line manager. At the outset of the engagement, we applied an adapted version of the executive onboarding effectiveness framework from Genesis/Egon Zehnder (International Institute for Management Development 2021).

The first building block is to diagnose the business situation and context. So, we sat down to reflect on the business situation and what would be the more visible context of the role. Many executive transition coaching clients come to appreciate times like this: where two partners come to explore, reflect, and come up with actions to tackle the first period of the transition. Many executives get sucked right into the realities of their business when they start. So, times of reflection and planning become even more precious.

The second building block involves taking charge of the newly inherited leadership team. This was delicate in many ways. For starters, Natalie's predecessor had been let go prematurely and before they were able to finish their multi-year tenure that had been an established practice at that firm. The other delicate situation involved the fact one of the leadership team members was a runner-up for the C-suite role and, despite entering the same process, was unsuccessful. This challenge surfaced sometime later when Natalie had formally started, and the unsuccessful leadership team member had quietly started to challenge the authority of Natalie by using team meetings and other opportunities to actively undermine her new boss. As part of the executive onboarding process, Natalie had undergone a leader assimilation process where the ground rules had been established subsequently.

Natalie confronted the team member in their 1:1 with their unhelpful behavior and reminded them of their jointly agreed team ground rules. Shortly after calling out the behavior of the team member, the individual left the firm. This was crucial as no leader should be putting up with such behavior. Furthermore, appearing to come across as indecisive or accommodating in situations like this can quickly undermine the newly appointed executive's authority and negatively impact their ability to deliver on the organization's strategy.

The third building block involves the executive's aligning with key stakeholders. This is a crucial step and is jointly agreed upon among all thought leaders in the onboarding and integrating arena. Together we used a comprehensive toolkit to identify key stakeholders (both internally and externally), look at their current versus ideal view of Natalie and their function, who would "own" that stakeholder, what would be key messages to land, at what frequency, and who would be responsible for preparation, delivery, and collecting feedback after engaging with them. Natalie suggested her business manager was involved in this process too. Subsequently, several key stakeholder interviews were conducted and no stone had been left unturned. Given the premature departure of Natalie's predecessor, this enabled Natalie to get a more in-depth understanding of the stakeholder landscape, the key priorities, and most importantly, what had been working well in the past and which areas and processes needed an overhaul or a complete revamp.

The fourth building block is about understanding and subsequently embracing the corporate culture. While this may look like an unnecessary step, given Natalie had been promoted internally, it would be a mistake to look at it that way. First, Natalie had made a cross-functional move. In any large, matrixed organization changing a business unit or region can at times feel like entering a new organization, let alone, a senior leader who gets appointed to the very top and at the same time must perform a cross-functional move. Second, moving from a country operation to the global head office is another sure sign for changes in the company culture, and what can be considered acceptable ways of working. Last, the firm had come under tremendous pressure externally for some visible management behaviors recently, so that added a layer of complexity to the company culture and what would be perceived as acceptable behavior, also externally speaking.

The last building block is for the executive to start shaping the strategic direction of the organization. This only becomes possible if the other four building blocks have been followed properly. Otherwise, the danger lies in the executive starting to shape the strategic direction of the company without having done the foundational work and possibly going wrong directionally as a result. As Stephen Covey, the famous author of the best-selling book *The 7 Habits of Highly Effective People*, once said, "Seek First to Understand, Then to Be Understood." Natalie had to first seek to understand the current state of her firm's environment, values, attitudes, relationships, and behaviors. She had to learn and use their vocabulary and honor their traditions.

IN SUMMARY

As you can see, while many of these building blocks and the framework may appear to be somewhat trivial initially, the devil lies in the details, and contextualizing these for the executive is key and crucial to the success. The advantage of working with an executive transition coach should be obvious by now. They combine the very best of transition advisers, so applying a structured framework, helping the executive to map stakeholders and map their first 90–120 days while also focusing on the mid- and long-term items that require more than a first ninety-day plan—including assessing existing leader and team competencies, styles, and behaviors, supporting the leader with self-awareness and behavior adjustments, and working with the leader over an extended period, typically around twelve months.

In the next chapter, I am going to look at organizational onboarding frameworks and how they can help or hinder executive transitions.

CHAPTER 5

ORGANIZATIONAL ONBOARDING FRAMEWORKS

———

When was the last time you were seriously impressed by an executive onboarding process? If you have to think about it, that may be an answer in itself.

UNDERWHELMING EXECUTIVE EXPERIENCE

During my time in Human Resources, I remember many instances where I was observing and applying what the organization had put in place to onboard executive leaders. More often than not, I felt underwhelmed by that process. From a lack of accountability to a process that had no clear ownership, to many more instances where the onboarding process mainly centered around administrative and legal compliance. I've probably seen it all.

But don't take my word for it. In 2017, a global survey conducted by Egon Zehnder/Genesis Advisers, 198 Human Resources executives assessed their organization's onboarding efforts (Byford, Watkins, and Triantogiannis 2017; Triantogiannis and Byford 2017). Most thought their company did a good job with basic orientation such as administrative arrangements (88 percent), business orientation (86 percent), and the legal and procedural formalities (85 percent) of signing up new hires.

Only half (52 percent) said their organizations were effective at aligning expectations with teams and their bosses. A third (33 percent) said they actively organized meetings with stakeholders. Less than a third (29 percent) said they facilitated culture familiarization. Genesis Advisers and Egon Zehnder documented robust integration of executive hires can shorten time to productivity from six months down to three to four (Byford, Watkins, and Triantogiannis 2017; Triantogiannis and Byford 2017). This can be achieved, for instance, through support provided by an executive coach who specializes in transitions.

A joint study from the Institute of Executive Development (IED) and Alexcel Group found *it takes more than six months for a new executive to be successfully integrated* (Gaines-Ross 2002). There are, however, variances between internal and external hires as we can see from the next image.

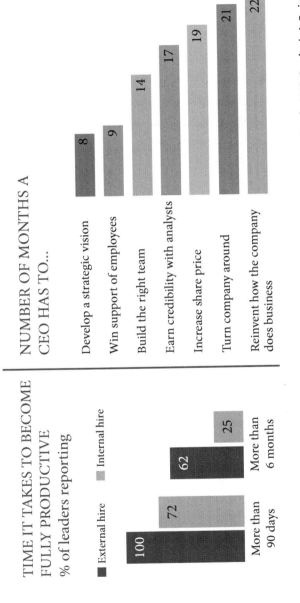

TIME IT TAKES TO BECOME FULLY PRODUCTIVE
% of leaders reporting

- External hire
- Internal hire

	External hire	Internal hire
More than 90 days	100	72
More than 6 months	62	25

NUMBER OF MONTHS A CEO HAS TO...

Develop a strategic vision	8
Win support of employees	9
Build the right team	14
Earn credibility with analysts	17
Increase share price	19
Turn company around	21
Reinvent how the company does business	22

Figure 5.1. Time it takes to be fully productive—% of leaders reporting. In the 2002 book, *CEO Capital: A Guide to Building CEO Reputation and Company Success*. Recreated with permission from Leslie Gaines-Ross in 2021.

In Chapter 2, we learned pace and magnitude of change are constantly rising in the business world, so it is no surprise senior-executive transitions are increasingly common.

A REALITY CHECK

Organizational changes reflect what's happening in the marketplace and in the world at large. Consider in 1997, Microsoft introduced the last version of Microsoft Office to the market on 55 floppy discs. In 1998, Apple brought out the first iMac without a floppy disc drive, and in 2008 it brought out the first MacBook Air without a CD drive. For over a decade, much of an organization's data is hosted in a Cloud solution (Microsoft Corporation 2014; Steeber 2018; Grothaus 2010).

Hand on heart: When was the last time you and your organization significantly transformed the executive onboarding process, moving from basic orientation to accelerated transition? To use this analogy, is your organization still stuck on floppy discs or CD ROMs? Or have you made the transition to the Cloud?

During my interview with Erik Schmidt, Chief HR Officer at Pandora, he referred to one of the executive onboarding experiences he has had:

> *It's really hard to think of a previous executive integration as a world-class benchmark, especially when many roles I've held have been new roles. One thing is true... if there is no structured executive onboarding in place, the reality of the role consumes time pretty quickly. So, it is crucial to attend to this early if circumstances allow.*

A positive example for a robust onboarding program to cite here is BAT. Richard Demblon, Chief HR Officer at Inchcape Shipping Services and former HR director with BAT, refers to his experience of over twelve years working for BAT during our interview:

> *The important thing was understanding what was necessary for anyone coming into the roles that you recruited outside, and then obviously there was a very good understanding of what you want to do. Here is pre-boarding, here is the onboarding induction pack, which is very clear, this is what we want to do, this is what the company is, and this is the whole FMCG (Fast Moving Consumer Goods) corporate culture. So, they do it very well, and you either fitted into that or you didn't. The BAT culture was very much where you fitted in and you were part of the family, or not, but there was an expectation of what was needed to get things done.*

Demblon also shares an example that is more in line with the majority of the respondents stating they lack proper process and support from their organizations:

> *When I went back into mining as the group HR director for Avocet Mining, they didn't have a people agenda. So, you're coming into an organization that has a very people administrative focus without a clear understanding.*

> *Well, where are we going from a strategic perspective, what are we trying to get out? And the onboarding aspect, very clear. You know what you want to do when*

you come in. This is what we have to achieve, and this is how we're going to do it. When you land, you spend the first two to three months trying to understand what it is that the company actually needs from you. What are you trying to deliver? Where is the people impact? So, the learning from that is having the luxury of our company DNA that pretty much is everything molded, thrown a lot of money behind it, and made sure that there is a common message and formula for driving to win.

There isn't much you do as a senior executive when coming into a new role. Then you waste a little bit of time trying to understand what it is that's needed, what are we trying to achieve? So your first four weeks are understanding the business, the people, how hard can you drive. And operationally from an HR perspective, there are always quick wins. How do you implement it, where are we wasting time? How can I automate some processes to try and drive efficiency, etc.?

Ultimately, as an HR leader, you want to wear the business hat first of all. You say, well, how's the organization going to evolve? What can we do more efficiently, and effectively? Where are the gaps in the leadership or the skills we currently have? You can then start reading where the business needs are and think: This is what I need to drive, and therefore, you start influencing and setting a direction.

The learning in these two examples is that it is easier if there's a clear framework, you come in and you carry on delivering.

SUPPORT AS A CRUCIAL FACTOR

A McKinsey & Company study surveyed 1,195 C-suite leaders on the level of transition support they received from their organizations (Chandran, de la Boutetiere, and Dewar 2015). Only 27 percent of the respondents believed their organizations had the right resources or programs in place to support their move into a C-level role. What's interesting is the responses from executives who made successful transitions (those who say they successfully aligned others during their transition and have successfully met their overall objectives) propose support has indeed a key role to play. These executives are twice as likely as all others to say they had received appropriate company support.

This is surprising, as a DDI study found there are six clear measures as to how an organization can support an incoming executive, whether internally promoted or externally hired (Development Dimensions International 2021).

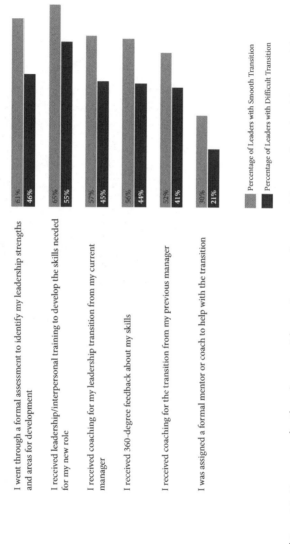

HOW ORGANIZATIONAL SUPPORT IMPACT EXECUTIVE TRANSITIONS

I went through a formal assessment to identify my leadership strengths and areas for development — 61% / 46%

I received leadership/interpersonal training to develop the skills needed for my new role — 65% / 55%

I received coaching for my leadership transition from my current manager — 57% / 45%

I received 360–degree feedback about my skills — 56% / 44%

I received coaching for the transition from my previous manager — 52% / 41%

I was assigned a formal mentor or coach to help with the transition — 30% / 21%

Percentage of Leaders with Smooth Transition

Percentage of Leaders with Difficult Transition

Figure 5.2. How organizational support impacts executive transitions. In "Leadership Transitions Report 2021," Global Leadership Forecast Series. Reproduced with permission from Development Dimensions International, 2021.

DISADVANTAGED INTERNAL PROMOTIONS

Another striking fact is the difference in the support that is provided to executives who have been promoted internally versus those who have been hired externally into similar level roles. A 2016 study by Michael Watkins found that at the executive level 56 percent of surveyed executives disagree or strongly disagree that their organization did a good job in supporting them during their "inboarding" (the onboarding of an executive who has been internally promoted into a new role).

There might be a belief in some organizations given that these are internal promotions, and as experienced executives, they don't need any support. Looking at the data that Michael Watkins has mined, they suggest roughly two thirds of all executive transitions are inboarding cases, i.e., internal promotions (Watkins 2016). When effectively supported, not only are the potential benefits for the executive leader obvious but also there are organizational benefits to gain as well.

THE IRONY OF PROCESS OPTIMIZATIONS

I have observed another unfortunate development over the years working in Human Resources. While many organizations have improved their overall onboarding process for *all* employees, few have made such improvements in the onboarding of their executive leaders.

So ironically, the improvements for all employees such as having a working laptop, email address, being set up in directories, having access to SharePoint or intranet and internal resources, doing the legal compliance training, and so forth seem to have ironed out the onboarding issues for most of the population. And often the same or a very similar process is applied to the executive level. However, this seems to have been achieved at the expense of the most senior leaders, who arguably are critical to the mission and success of that same organization too.

During an online panel discussion organized by Russell Reynolds Associates, Ernest Marshall, executive VP HR at Eaton Corporation, referred to this when speaking about his own onboarding experience, which wasn't particularly great (Marshall 2021). As the most senior HR leader of the organization, he's got a keen desire to get this right so others wouldn't have to go through the same mediocre experience. Here's how he described Eaton Corporation's organizational onboarding practice:

> For us, we just hired a new CFO and chief technology officer and a general counsel all during this (pandemic) period. We had put together a more formalistic onboarding plan because when I arrived, I got a sheet of paper and they said go for it. You know, it was important for me to say when we bring people into the organization, how do we help, how do we give them a leg up as much as we can.
>
> In the onboarding process you have to be incredibly intentional, irrespective of a COVID-19 environment. The other day I said to my team we should always think about our onboarding as if it took place during a pandemic because you have to be much more intentional.
>
> So what do we do when we bring people on? For the first week we have individuals and group calls set, and

we do try to be intentional with how we connect. What we do on the back end is to go and ask people, how did you feel? How was that experience? What would you do differently if you could change it? Because we're trying to get the dialogue going, we're always trying to improve the process.

The folks that we've brought in have been very complimentary around how we've set them up and got them established. Now think about it. We're in seventy-five countries. So you've got time zones, you've got languages, you've got leaders where most of their team are in different parts of the world, and so they've got to figure out a way to connect, and so we try to bridge that gap. We help them with their thirty-, sixty-, and ninety-day plan. We do a new manager assimilation upfront. We've learned how to do these virtually, and then we do another assimilation about a year out just to make sure that we're connected as well.

I'm always asking for insight and feedback if someone is doing something better because I'll steal shamelessly if there's a good idea. Steal with pride, absolutely (Marshall 2021).

VALUE BEING DESTROYED

Note a staggering **$166 billion** is spent annually on leadership development in the USA alone. The global figure is estimated to be around **$366 billion** (Westfall 2019). How much of this is spent on executive transitions versus learning management systems (LMS) that have outdated content and low usage?

In another study conducted by Russell Reynolds Associates, they found that roughly 90 percent of the cost of making an executive hire is spent upfront in their hiring—with only 10 percent or less spent on making that same hire successful (Dineen 2021). It appears as if organizations are spending substantial amounts of money to hire the best candidate, but then leave them to sink or swim when they are on board.

Rudi Kindts, former CHRO at BAT and now himself an executive coach, reflected on what often happens in corporate environments and the lack of structured tools to identify passions and preferences *before* executive appointments are made during our interview:

> *Sometimes we go through transitions blindly. We need tools to understand what makes us tick. And we need to look at how we can eventually create the environment to transition in line with what motivates us and where we're going to be able to use our strengths. There are so many of these examples. As a coach, I observe so many unhappy transitions because I think often there are so many blind spots. The focus is usually not on the emotion, it's on the career. It's not about wow, what does it for me? So those were some of the things that I overlooked, and I see being overlooked. Getting transitions right would make a big difference.*

In the next chapter, I will explore the top ten reasons for executive transition failure and how to avoid them.

CHAPTER 6

THE TOP 10 REASONS FOR EXECUTIVE TRANSITION FAILURE

———

Before we get into the reasons why executive transitions are a failure about 40 percent of the time, let's take a quick look at what I have often found to be top of mind for the newly appointed executive (Keller and Meaney 2018).

TRANSITIONING EXECUTIVE'S TOP CONCERNS

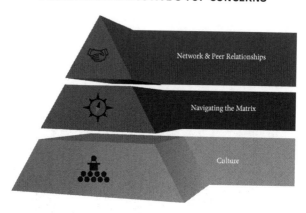

Figure 6.1. The transitioning executive's top three concerns, created by Navid Nazemian Executive Coaching in 2021.

Each time when starting in a new executive role, I thought very carefully about the new network and relationships I had to build, particularly with my new line manager, peers, and direct reports. Furthermore, I was very mindful of the delicate task of having to navigate what is often a complex matrix organization. Last, but not least, I often had concerns around the culture of the new organization, especially when I was hired externally. I also know of many other executives who had a long tenure in their previous organization and just weren't sure how culturally adaptable they would be in a new company.

FAILING ORGANIZATION STRATEGIES

When was the last time you witnessed a new organization's strategy execution fall apart?

Strategy execution is one of the most crucial elements of successful organizations simply because there is no value in having the greatest strategy in the world if it isn't being executed properly. Yet, many organizations fail to get it right. *Harvard Business Review* finds the majority of strategies fail due to poor execution (Carucci 2017).

This exceptionally high failure rate is shocking, especially if one considers all large companies use external strategy consulting firms often in tandem with fully staffed in-house strategy teams to define and articulate their strategy before starting to implement them.

MANY REASONS FOR FAILURE

According to executives interviewed confidentially during a ten-year longitudinal study on executive leadership, the main reason for this high failure rate (61 percent) was executives not being properly prepared for strategic challenges they had to face at the time of their appointment, a classic case of executive overwhelm (Carucci 2017).

Arguably, the work required to craft and execute company strategy is exceptionally difficult. As a result, executives may be tempted to oversimplify, dilute, or match this to their competency level accordingly.

One effective way to avoid the high cost of failed strategy execution is to prepare the executives for the real requirements of their roles. It would bring the failure rate down and give the organization a chance to adapt to the external circumstances and, ultimately, thrive.

A 2009 *Financial Times* article by Brooke Masters quotes Kevin Kelly, former CEO of the executive search company Heidrick & Struggles: "We've found that 40% of executives hired at the senior level are pushed out, fail, or quit within 18 months."

It's expensive in terms of lost revenue. It's expensive in terms of the individual's hiring. It's damaging to morale. The Institute of Executive Development (IED) in Palo Alto, California, USA, and the Alexcel Group have similar findings in their "Executive Transitions" study (Wheeler 2008):

- 30 percent of external executive hires fail within two years.
- 23 percent of internal executive transfers fail within two years.
- Ramp-up time for new external hires ranges from six to nine months.
- Ramp-up time for internal transfers ranges from three to nine months.

CEO DEPARTURES

When companies announce their CEOs are leaving, they may offer any number of vague reasons, but rarely would they say the chief executive was "fired" or explain precisely why. There is an element of shame, both for the organization admitting that despite their best efforts the CEO didn't work out, as well as for the CEO who simply didn't do their job successfully. Whatever the actual reason, another study suggests in the past two years, 52 percent of announced CEO departures from companies on the Russell 3000 Index were likely the result of executives being shown the door (Keller and Meaney 2018). That includes those who say they resigned, stepped down, "just felt the time was right to leave," or had a sudden urge to spend more time with family.

McKinsey cites several research papers suggesting two years after executive transitions, between 27 percent to 46 percent of them are regarded as "failures or disappointments" (Keller and Meaney 2018). Leaders rank organizational politics as the main challenge, and 67 percent of leaders wish they had moved faster to change the culture. Bearing in mind all of the above studies, nearly half of executive transitions fail (Keller and Meaney 2018).

That being said, the speed with which executives have to bring about change and transformation is crucial. Timing is key as we learned in Chapter 2. Moving too fast may result in organ rejection and moving too slowly may mean the leader fails to deliver what's expected of them. George Bradt rightly points out the leader should conform to the organizational culture first instead of trying to change it until they have "earned that right" (Bradt 2012a).

These matters aren't problems only for leaders who come in from the outside; 79 percent of external and 69 percent of internal hires report implementing culture change is difficult (Goldsmith 2008).

If all of the above didn't convince you, let me share one more study showing why the 40 percent failure rate is pretty accurate. A study by Manchester, Inc.—often attributed to The Center for Creative Leadership—found 40 percent of leaders going into new roles fail (Bradt 2021b; Fisher 2021). Brad Smart has cited a failure rate of 50 percent in his 2005 book,

Topgrading: How To Hire, Coach and Keep A Players. Leadership IQ published a study suggesting the failure rate of managers is 46 percent within eighteen months (Murphy 2005). *Harvard Business Review* cites "that 50%–60% of executives fail within the first 18 months of being promoted or hired" (Carucci 2017).

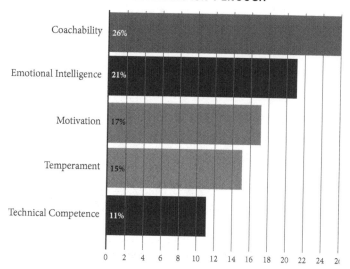

HBR: ONBOARDING ISN'T ENOUGH

Figure 6.2. The real reasons for executive transition failure. Reproduced with permission from Mark Murphy, Leadership IQ: Why New Hires Fail (Emotional Intelligence vs. Skills) (Murphy 2005).

Bear in mind these are leaders who demonstrated success and showed intelligence, initiative, and results in their previous roles. One of my interview partners, Anton Fishman, referred to the 40 percent in our interview as follows:

Now, I know you didn't want to talk about the sort of research that time and time again says up to 40% of senior executive appointments either fail or disappoint the organization. But that research I first came across it in the nineties, and I saw it replicated in the early 2000s. It's probably being replicated now. It is pretty consistent.

I have personally studied many of these research papers that have analyzed the top reasons for executive transition failures. I have added to these my observations from five large multinational companies I have worked for, enriched with survey data from running masterclasses and working with senior executives on their transition. So, I'd like to share with you my meta-analysis of the top ten reasons why executive transitions fail about 40 percent of the time (Keller and Meaney 2018).

TOP 10 REASONS FOR EXECUTIVE FAILURE
As you can see the organizational environment for newly appointed executives can be tricky and sometimes even contradicting and confusing. Now let's look at more granular reasons for executive failure:

META STUDY OF THE TOP 10 REASONS FOR EXECUTIVE FAILURES

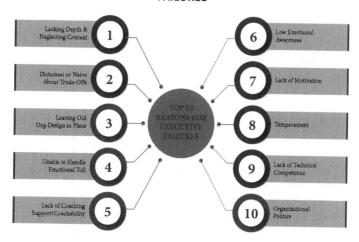

Figure 6.3. The top ten reasons for executive transition failure. Combined from two independent studies that were conducted by Leadership IQ & Navalent (Murphy 2005; Carucci 2017).

Two separate studies from Leadership IQ and Navalent (a consulting firm cofounded by Rob Carucci) lay out, independent of each other, why executive transitions are a failure about 40 percent of the time (Murphy 2005; Carucci 2017). I will explain these and provide examples below.

REASON 1: LACKING DEPTH AND NEGLECTING CONTEXT

This becomes an issue when the executive is heavily internally focused and lacking an outside-in perspective, sometimes because there are cultural or process issues that require attention. This is particularly common in turnaround situations and when the business isn't doing great.

REASON 2: DISHONEST OR NAIVE ABOUT TRADE-OFFS

This is when the executive is either naive or dishonest about some of the trade-offs they have to make, sometimes quite early on. Some of the questions I have seen executive coaching clients grappling with are:

"Can I make those one to two upgrades to my leadership team?"
"How quickly can I move ahead with that?"
"What would the organization think if I did that?"
"How would that potentially become my reputation?"
"How much of a tight rein is acceptable here?"

REASON 3: LEAVING THE OLD ORGANIZATION DESIGN IN PLACE

This may be because the executive doesn't want to make the tough calls early on since it could unnecessarily ruffle feathers. Or it could be the executive's conflict management style is such that they would prefer to play it safe and shy away from conflict. Experience shows if the executive hasn't made the tough calls during an acceptable period (during the first three months in a new role, according to Russell Reynolds Associates), chances are these won't become easier to tackle later (Dineen 2021). My experience suggests timing is critical here. Making big changes too early could prove costly and wrong as the executive may not have enough information to base their decision on. Waiting for too long would also make the change most likely trickier and the messaging around why a change may be needed will be harder to land.

REASON 4: UNABLE TO HANDLE EMOTIONAL TOLL

Some executives are simply not able to do it. We will cover this later in the book, but let me give it away here briefly: The stress levels associated with an executive transition are north of the stress people face when they are going through a divorce or significant health issues. Just imagine the case of an executive who has been cross-functionally promoted, moving from one country to another, having a big promotion, and joining a new organization. While technically this is a single transition, it involves five major executive transition challenges. As a result, the emotional toll coming at the executive will be enormous.

REASON 5: LACK OF COACHING SUPPORT OR COACHABILITY

This is about the lack of coaching support by the executive's organization. Let's remember the data from Russell Reynolds Associates: 90 percent of the cost that goes into an executive hire is spent on the assessment and selection process. This involves screening and engaging a head hunter, screening profiles, going through the candidate long list, agreeing on a shortlist, interviewing shortlisted candidates and sometimes a diagnostic assessment (Dineen 2021b).

And less than 10 percent goes into onboarding and ultimately making sure the executive is fully supported (e.g., by an executive transition coach) once they have been hired (Dineen 2021a). Given the 10 percent is an average figure, it is likely in some cases that the spend is zero on the executive's onboarding and support. So, the onboarding process for the executive is essentially the same for any new joiner. They get a laptop, a working email, a personal assistant (PA), and are told good luck. Then the executive's PA will need to schedule a few random meetings for them and identify the stakeholders to meet with. By the way, here comes the annual report and our strategy document, so make sure you read them.

REASON 6: LOW EMOTIONAL AWARENESS

Daniel Goleman's seminal book, *Emotional Intelligence*, was published over twenty-five years ago in 1995. Since then, a whole range of different assessment and diagnostic instruments, books, and leadership development training has been introduced to the market to increase the EQ of executive leaders. Not to mention, many leadership development coaches have specialized in this area.

In more practical terms, this is the executive who may struggle to "read" the boardroom. Let's face it, if an executive doesn't possess high levels of emotional intelligence and isn't great at reading the boardroom during normal times, the pandemic won't have increased their chances of reading the boardroom through a tile on their screen. They will most likely struggle if they have transitioned during the pandemic as reading through a tile on the screen is most certainly not easier than doing it in real life in a face-to-face situation.

REASON 7: LACK OF MOTIVATION

Executive sponsors can be tough, and so can internal stakeholders. What executives often have to face also are mixed messages. I've observed this particular issue many times when working with executive transition coaching clients. Well-intended but contradictory advice is delivered to executives by their line manager, the chairman, their C-suite HR or finance leader, the executive board, etc. Ironically, these mixed messages sometimes come from the same source! Some of the most common examples Sean Dineen refers to during an online webinar are:

"You must challenge your peers and the organization." vs. "Simply follow the playbook."
"You must score points early on; go for quick wins that are visible." vs. "Take your time to learn and be a fly on the wall."
"You must demonstrate your independence as an executive." vs. "Make sure you always ask for help and support." (Dineen 2021b)

Another case is when the executive has done their research and homework, and when they think they have a good understanding of the organization upon joining. Then, reality bites. Nothing comes even close to what the executive thought the organization, the executive team, and the board would be like when they agreed to join. As a result, the executive loses traction, and with that, they start to lose motivation.

REASON 8: TEMPERAMENT

Showing too much of your emotions at work or no emotions at all can both be fatal. This is particularly an issue when the executive's temperament and that of the organization and their executive leadership team are fundamentally different. Just think of the different levels of temperament between Bill Gates and Steve Ballmer. Now imagine Satya Nadella next to Steve Ballmer and how their temperaments differ. Arguably all three have been successful when leading Microsoft as CEO, but looking at the same at GE, the picture is a different one.

Jack Welch led GE from 1981 to 2001 and increased its market value from $12 billion to $410 billion when he retired (Craighill 2020). On the other hand, Jeff Immelt, who took over from him, managed abysmal returns to the shareholders, with GE's stock ending lower than when he assumed the reins in September 2001 (Gara 2017). Even when counting dividends, GE's stock returned 27 percent under Immelt, so a bit more than 1.5 percent annually, versus a whopping 183 percent gain by the Dow Jones Industrial Average, or the equivalent of a 7.6 percent annual return. Versus competitors, Emerson Electric, Honeywell International, Siemens, and ABB, GE's performance lagged even more. Excluding dividends, GE shares were off roughly by 20 percent (Gara 2017).

REASON 9: LACK OF TECHNICAL COMPETENCE

Interestingly enough, this is only ranked number nine in the top ten reasons for executive failure. The reason is it accounts for about 11 percent of the total cases (Watkins 2019). Some might argue this is too high given all the due diligence and executive search-related bells and whistles attached to an executive hire. Such search mandates are often supported by the top search firms who have a deep expertise in this area including referencing and cross-referencing executive-level candidates to avoid trouble once they join an organization. This reason for failure may be due to cross-industry moves or context when a learned skill doesn't necessarily apply to the new role.

REASON 10: ORGANIZATIONAL POLITICS

Last but certainly not least, reason number ten for executive failure is down to organizational politics. The irony is most organizations claim to have no or very little evidence of it. Yet, whoever has work experience in the global headquarters of a large organization will have come across this. Sometimes it is one of the so-called "elephants in the room" nobody would like to admit or talk about, but it's an elephant that's probably trampled all over us and left us with bruises.

Note these are the top ten reasons for executive failure, according to the studies conducted by Leadership IQ and Navalent. In reality, there are many more reasons.

MACRO EVENTS

What I haven't deliberately covered are external macro events. Arguably they are mostly outside of the executive's control. During our interview, Erik Schmidt, Chief HR Officer of Pandora, shared an example when he had to wind down and leave a business a few months after September 11:

> I had an early career experience; it was quite a wake-up call. This was not just straightforward like apply for a job, get it, and start working...off you go in there. No matter how well you plan and you're in your ninety-day period (into your executive transition), there are going to be things that come along you will never foresee that can have a dramatic effect on your (career) trajectory. That was one story which I learned from and went on from there.

It may be hard to remember ten things at the same time; therefore, I have grouped these into three reasons for executive failure: culture, people, and politics. Interestingly, all of these are related to the nature of the work and the support

HR delivers in an organization. My personal observation is getting the new company culture and the timing of its change wrong is probably the main reason why executives often fail during their transition.

TOP 3 GROUPED REASONS FOR EXECUTIVE FAILURES

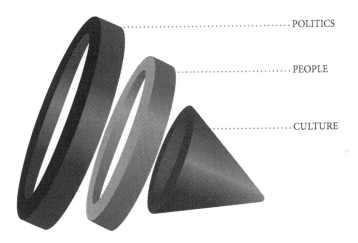

Figure 6.4. The top three grouped reasons for executive transition failure, created by Navid Nazemian Executive Coaching in 2021.

In the next chapter, I'll lay out the true cost of failed executive transitions.

CHAPTER 7

THE TRUE COST OF FAILED EXECUTIVE TRANSITIONS

—

The impact of failed executive transitions isn't negligible. Corporate Executive Board (CEB) research suggests unsuccessful transitions result in 15 percent lower performance and lower employee engagement, with team members 20 percent more likely to be disengaged or to leave the organization. The flip side of this is 90 percent of leadership teams whose executive leader had a successful transition go on to achieve their three-year performance goals. In those teams, the attrition risk is 13 percent lower than the rest (Keller and Meaney 2018).

PROMINENT CEO TRANSITION FAILURES

Now let's take a brief look at some of the prominent CEO transition failures during the last years, how long they stayed in the role, and what their severance pay packages were.

Bear in mind the numbers cited below don't include the long-term share awards, so-called "Golden Hello" (or "Golden Parachute" if you're based in the US) or a new joiner bonus, pre-agreed pension contributions, and many more pay components. Hence why we look at the cost of executive transition failure to be around 2.5 to twenty times the executive's salary data later (Fatemi 2016; Nawaz 2017). Other research suggests the true cost of failed executive onboarding can be as high as thirty times the executive's salary (Stoddard and Wyckoff 2008).

CHIEF EXECUTIVE OFFICER
SALARY LEVELS BY MARKET CAPITALISATION

Market capitalisation	No of co's	LOWER DECILE £	LOWER QUARTILE £	MEDIAN £	UPPER QUARTILE £	UPPER DECILE £	AVERAGE £
£4-6bn	26	524,600	568,100	807,000	874,000	961,600	743,900
£6-8bn	19	587,600	672,500	760,000	850,800	971,000	766,000
£8-17bn	22	631,700	714,600	854,500	978,400	1,078,200	849,500
£17-36bn	14	975,100	1,007,400	1,136,000	1,267,300	1,364,900	1,137,800
>£36bn	13	1,072,400	1,199,200	1,284,000	1,300,000	1,324,200	1,238,800

Figure 7.1. Chief executive officer salary levels by market capitalization. Table recreated from "Your guide, Directors" remuneration in FTSE 250 companies (Deloitte 2020).

C-SUITE TRANSITION FAILURE #1

Jennifer Morgan left SAP only months after the German software giant made her co-CEO and the first woman to head a company on Germany's DAX index. Christian Klein took over solo after what was previously hailed for decades as a proven leadership model. The company blamed the coronavirus. She received a severance payment of $1,970,900 (Wallmine 2021).

C-SUITE TRANSITION FAILURE #2

Leo Apotheker: On September 22, 2011, the Hewlett Packard (HP) board of directors replaced Apotheker as chief executive, effective immediately, with fellow board member and former eBay chief Meg Whitman. Apotheker served barely ten months and received over $13 million in compensation, a severance payment of $7.2 million, shares worth $3.56 million, and a performance bonus of $2.4 million, although the company lost more than $30 billion in market capitalization during his tenure (Stoddard and Wyckoff 2008).

C-SUITE TRANSITION FAILURE #3

For a while, Boeing just couldn't catch a breath when it came to chief executives. In 2003, CEO Phil Condit resigned amid allegations the company had stolen documents from its competitors. Boeing replaced Condit by bringing back Harry Stonecipher, who had retired from the company in 2002. However, Stonecipher didn't last long. It's arguably the safest bet one can imagine to bring back a retired CEO from the same company; however, Stonecipher's second tenure as

CEO only lasted a year and three months with a payout of $1.8 million (Weinmann 2011).

C-SUITE TRANSITION FAILURE #4

Uber president Jeff Jones quit after only six months in the role. He tweeted about his resignation instead of telling the founder who had appointed him: "I joined Uber because of its mission and the challenge to build global capabilities that would help the company mature and thrive long-term. It is now clear, however, that the beliefs and approach to leadership that have guided my career are inconsistent with what I saw and experienced at Uber, and I can no longer continue as president of the ride-sharing business. There are thousands of amazing people at the company, and I truly wish everyone well" (Isaac 2017).

Here is Uber founder Travis Kalanick's slightly startled full note that was issued to staff worldwide:

> *Team,*
> *I wanted to let you know that Jeff Jones has decided to resign from Uber.*
> *Jeff joined Uber in October 2016 from being CMO at retailer Target. In 6 months, he made an important impact on the company—from his focus on being driver obsessed to delivering our first brand reputation study, which will help set our course in the coming months and year.*
> *After we announced our intention to hire a COO, Jeff came to the tough decision that he doesn't see his future at Uber. It is unfortunate that this was announced*

through the press but I thought it was important to send
all of you an email before providing comment publicly.
Rachel, Pierre and Mac will continue to lead the Global
Ops teams, reporting to me until we have signed a COO.
Troy Stevenson, who leads CommOps, and Shalin Amin
who leads brand design will report to Rachel Holt. Ab
Gupta will report to Andrew MacDonald.
Thanks,
Travis (Isaac 2017)

C-SUITE TRANSITION FAILURE #5

Another instance I vividly recall was when the chairman of an organization I was a member of decided to install a new chief executive officer (CEO). The firm had been running very successfully with a managing director (MD) for years when this decision was made. As there had never been a CEO structure in that firm, the dual leadership created a considerable amount of confusion, first among the firm's staff, then with key accounts as to what that meant for the existing MD and for the incoming CEO, who was brought in with much hoopla.

The newly formed duo had to set up conference calls to explain to the staff and to associates how the two roles would be complementary and not substituting one another, and how it would work in practice. The newly established CEO would be focusing on strategy and the existing MD would be focusing on the execution of the strategy and managing client relationships. In conversations with staff and clients, the new CEO hailed the long-established heritage and successes of the firm, but also shared quite disruptive ideas at the same time.

While on the conference call, I could literally sense how early it was for that CEO to make those claims about the firm and the desired culture changes. He also spoke about the successes of consulting firms and business units he had led before. If he had paid close attention, he should have picked up how several members were raising their eyebrows hearing the CEO speak about the firm's culture. As discussed in the previous chapter, getting the culture element wrong is one of the biggest mistakes an incoming executive can make. Getting the timing right is essential. Too early, and the staff won't believe the credibility of the messenger. Embarking on culture change too late will become an uphill battle to change any aspect of it.

It wasn't long, however, before all those disruptive ideas and the tenure of the newly established CEO had to end abruptly. All of this took place in less than six months. The newly established CEO moved on very quickly to another firm. The MD became the leader at the helm of that firm again, and the board did not establish a new CEO after that.

INCREASINGLY SHORTER CEO LIFESPANS

Russell Reynolds Associates points out another unfortunate trend in the S&P 500 companies in the study's period between 2003 to 2015 (O'Kelley 2018). Among these five hundred companies, there were 688 CEO transitions over the twelve-years with 40 percent of the organizations experiencing two or more CEO transitions. The average CEO tenure was 5.9 years during the same time period.

Their findings suggest one in every seven CEO retirements in the S&P 500 was followed by the forced and surprising departure of the new CEO within the first three years of being appointed. A staggering 85 percent of these were due to reasons such as low performance, or they were simply forced out by the management board or activist investors (O'Kelley 2018).

The author of the study rightly points out that given the cost and investment that usually goes into CEO appointments of large, publicly listed companies, these are expensive misses (O'Kelley 2018). Every CEO departure carried financial consequences and lost business opportunities.

Another study by PwC found organizations that are left with no other choice than to fire their CEO relinquish an average of $1.8 billion in shareholder value compared with those that have an orderly succession plan, irrespective of whether the replacement CEO is an insider or outsider (Favaro, Karlsson, and Neilson 2015). The authors of the study also note companies that experienced unplanned successions "would have generated, on average, an estimated $112 billion more in market value in the year before and the year after their turnover if their CEO succession had been the result of planning" (Favaro, Karlsson, and Neilson 2015).

The enormous cost of failed executive transitions was also confirmed by another study from Ward Howell International (Shekshnia and Osnes 2019). The estimation of a failed succession can reduce revenues by 3 percent for a typical $1 billion revenue company, with further hits to the market capitalization of the same organization that runs into billions.

This only confirms earlier findings from a 2008 study by Stoddard and Wyckoff that puts a direct cost of failed CEO exits in the range of $12–$52 million depending on the size of the organization and total losses to the US economy north of $1 billion per year.

MASSIVE COST OF FAILURE

The massive cost of failed executive transitions is several-fold.

Let's look at the example of the average CEO salary in the UK for a company that is publicly listed with a market cap of £6–18 billion. According to the *Deloitte: Director's Remuneration in FTSE 100 Companies* 2020 report, this was on average £855,300 per annum. Applying the 2.5 to 30 times cost of failed transitions, it gets us anywhere from £2 to £25 million.

Deviating from the above example of a FTSE CEO, if the average executive in your organization makes about £250,000, you are still looking at a cost of about £625,000 to £7,500,000. What is even worse is the scenario where the executive chooses to stay, as there will be massive indirect costs involved, such as lower performance of the business unit, the opportunity cost of inaction, the cost of higher turnover of the teams, and so much more.

So far, we have covered the cost of a failed executive transition to an organization. Let's also remind ourselves the cost of a failure to an executive can be devastating, particularly if the failure is publicly acknowledged or known in an industry. Imagine the middle-aged CEO who fails to deliver early on in their new executive role.

What is going to be the impact on the future trajectory of their career? Would they be able to find another executive role? If they did, would it be at the same level and offer the same prospects for professional growth? How about the reward aspects? Will the package be better, similar, or much lower than what they are used to?

There is a real chance the executive doesn't land another appropriate level role and has to shift gears by moving into consulting/interim management or other activities as a result. One of the cases I know of is a senior executive who spent more than twenty years working for the same multinational organization, more than half of that time as an international assignee (expatriate). Once the executive was laid off as a result of an organization-wide restructuring, he never landed another executive role and had to retire before he turned fifty.

Let's face it, it may come as a surprise to some executives how lonely the top job can be. It may sound counter-intuitive at first. However, when executives are appointed into the C-suite, they are suddenly cut off from a lot of their fundamental mentorship and groups of people they used to deal with previously. Once they have made it to the top job, they don't have the same access to some of the people they used to. So, they find that it gets lonely pretty quickly.

There is another cost to look at when it comes to failed executive transitions, namely that of a development opportunity gap. According to a recent study from DDI, female leaders are missing key development support (Development Dimensions International 2021).

THE GENDER GAP IN EXECUTIVE TRANSITIONS

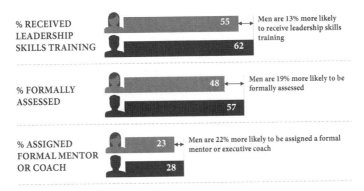

Figure 7.2. The gender gap in executive transitions in "Leadership Transition Report," Global Leadership Forecast Series. Reproduced with permission from Development Dimensions International, 2021.

The study has found female leaders are less likely to receive executive transition support than their male counterparts. Depending on the item that's been identified to support executive transitions, the gap ranges from 13 percent to 22 percent; hence, it is statistically significant. What strikes me is a formal mentor or executive transition coach is made available to only 23 percent to 28 percent of senior leaders (Development Dimensions International 2021). Yet, we know how crucial that support is to *all* transitioning executives.

This may be surprising as many organizations are responding to the changing market dynamics and are under pressure to build female leadership benches at all management levels. Partially, this is also driven by legislation in certain countries where the representation of the management board has legal requirements of a minimum representation by female leaders.

The DDI study also found there is a direct link between a long executive onboarding and the engagement level of the same executive, as we can see in the following chart displaying favorable responses (Development Dimensions International 2021).

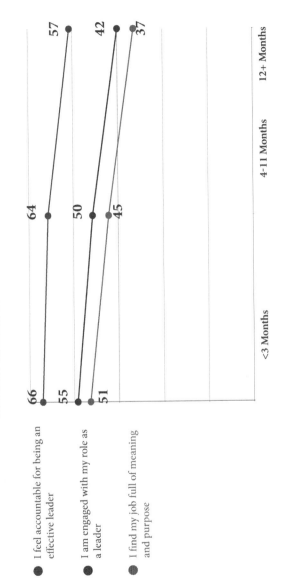

Figure 7.3. The cost of long executive transitions in "Leadership Transition Report," Global Leadership Forecast Series. Reproduced with permission from Development Dimensions International, 2021.

At the time of getting to the final stage of this book, I am based in London, England. So, let's look at the current makeup of executive directors in the FTSE 100. These are large, publicly listed companies in the United Kingdom. Here, we see the ratio of female executive committee members ranging from 23.1 percent in 2019 to 26.5 percent in 2020. If we look at the FTSE 250, we see 18.6 percent female executive committee representation in 2019 which has increased to 21.7 percent in 2020 (Wilson 2021).

When it comes to executive committee member appointments in the FTSE 100, the split in 2020 was 36 percent female versus 64 percent male. When looking at the FTSE 250 (mid- to large-cap) we find a similar picture of a split of 32 percent of executive committee appointments being female and 68 percent of them being male candidates (Wilson 2021).

In a nutshell, it is clear the current makeup of executive directors is anything but close to gender parity. What also becomes clear is very few organizations have made real progress in this area, and this makes the DDI study findings even more alarming.

In the next chapter, I'll focus on key executive transition challenges related to people and culture.

CHAPTER 8

KEY EXECUTIVE TRANSITION CHALLENGES: PEOPLE & CULTURE

When was the last time you saw a spectacular CEO failure that was related to people or culture? It is like watching an avalanche in slow motion. As terrible as it is to see something like that unfold, it is as tragic as it is an avoidable failure. Research demonstrates it occurs regularly. CEOs are no exception to the 40 percent failure rate (Keller and Meaney 2018).

In this chapter, we're going to focus on some of the most common people and culture challenges executives face when transitioning into a new role. The first eight have been identified by Michael D. Watkins, author of *The First 90 Days*. I have added four more challenges with which I have helped my executive coaching clients over the years to create the ultimate list of top executive transition challenges. I will also provide examples in each case to bring each transition challenge to life.

WHAT ARE THE MOST COMMON TYPES OF EXECUTIVE TRANSITIONS?

According to the 2019 book *Master Your Next Move* by Michael D. Watkins, there are eight common transition types. Note most moves to new leadership roles involve *multiple* types of transitions that often occur at the same time. The more types of transitions an executive experiences simultaneously, the greater the overall challenge will be.

MOST COMMON TYPES OF EXECUTIVE TRANSITION CHALLENGES

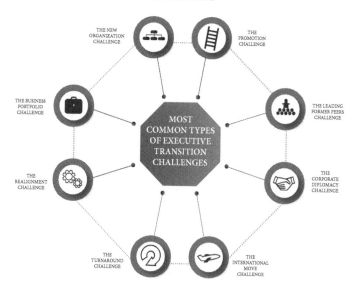

Figure 8.1. Common transition types and the corresponding challenges in *Master Your Next Move* (Watkins 2019).

For the sake of simplicity, I have broken down the top challenges into two categories. The first, people- and culture-related challenges, is covered in this chapter, while Chapter 9 will focus on business and technical challenges.

1. THE NEW ORGANIZATION CHALLENGE, OR HOW DOES WORK GET DONE AROUND HERE?

"I felt completely lost when I started my new role..."

That is a great question, and one I have had to grapple with over the years. I have worked in six sectors for five large multinational companies over the last twenty-five years.

Each time, I had to understand and adapt to a new organizational culture, master organizational politics, and identify and align with the expectations of a wide range of key stakeholders such as direct reports, line managers, peers, executive committee members, etc.

The same applies to my executive transition coaching clients who sometimes find it particularly hard to adjust and embrace a new organizational culture after a long tenure in a single organization. Remember when that long-term personal relationship came to an end and you started something new? In many ways, starting a new professional relationship is very similar. You have to adjust to the new personality and character and find out about shared beliefs and assumptions about how you should behave and interact with your new partner or organization. There is a particular stretch that is required when leaders are faced with this challenge; hence, it is a common and prominent executive transition challenge.

2. THE BIG PROMOTION CHALLENGE

"I was promoted beyond my competence levels..."

Being promoted one level up (sometimes two or even more) and understanding what needs to be done to be successful at the new level can include many things. I remember vividly how, over a decade ago—as an early in career employee—I was promoted to become the head of HR for a multinational operating company.

It was a role that had been offered to me three months prior, and one I had turned down then, saying I didn't feel ready for it, given it was a two-level promotion and came much earlier than was suggested to me when I was hired.

I eventually accepted, and as a member of the local executive committee, I had to represent our operating company on the Region's Board Compensation Committee, often referred to as the remuneration committee. This was in addition to many other responsibilities, which included overseeing the corporate security function, managing a fleet of company cars, and an onshore mobility service provider.

It was clear I did not possess much of the technical competencies at the expected level, so I had to dig deep to get to the desired and expected level of competence. While doing all of this, I had to ensure appropriate delegation focusing on the right priorities, develop and demonstrate leadership behaviors, and show a considerable amount of "executive presence." Next to the required technical skills, there were many emotions attached to this. Am I enough? Will I make it? Is it too early for such a big promotion? What if I don't live up to the expectation? Of course, some of these are related to the famous imposter syndrome. In fact, an estimated 70 percent of people experience these feelings at some point in their lives according to a review article in the *International Journal of Behavioral Science* (Sakulku 2011).

While gaining proficiency, I was supported by my functional line manager, my team, as well as a coach who helped me enormously through this professional transition period. The rest is history.

Rudi Kindts, ex-CHRO of BAT, shared with me his example of how he had gotten this wrong initially when he was appointed to the position of group Human Resources director and member of the executive committee. He received developmental feedback from his CEO when he asked for it as a newly appointed CHRO:

> *I had been operating within my comfort zone, by that I mean representing the HR function on an executive team, and not much more. I was leading and interacting in accordance with that and where I allocated my work time. So, I spent a lot of time with the HR team and with my HR leadership team members. In all of this, if I look at my allocation of time horizontally up, compared to the time spent vertically down, it was out of sync.*

In short, the CEO feedback suggested he had to spend more time with the executive committee *as a member of that team*—and not just as the HR representative. The role was wider, and deeper, than he'd conceived.

3. THE LEADING-FORMER-PEERS CHALLENGE— SOUNDS STRAIGHTFORWARD, RIGHT?
"I didn't know what to do or how to behave..."

At one stage in my career, a member of our team and I had to go through a structured selection process that had been organized by our colleagues in Human Resources. At the end of that lengthy and grueling process, I was selected to lead the team of (mostly) former peers.

This meant I had to suddenly manage my former peers as a line manager, tread lightly at first, and be mindful of not introducing major overhauls right away.

One of the best decisions I took early was to set up a new schedule for team and individual meetings, set up our team ground rules in a team session, and explain my expectations for communication in our team.

That being said, at times I did have to exert authority and provide direction. In the end, the new leader cannot be the same as a peer. So, what became clear to me was I could not have close, personal friendships with my former peers. In a way that was the hardest part, as it is inherently part of the deal and probably a loss for everybody, but how else was I supposed to avoid coming across as playing favorites?

This changed our team dynamic quite dramatically, not least because one of my peers also had high hopes of landing that role. Understandably, she was disappointed. I would have been, too. So, I had to deal with a disappointed peer of mine who went through that emotional process.

I made sure to let her know I did value her and I would have been equally disappointed if it had been me, and I, nevertheless, would have respected her if she had landed that role. In the end, we managed to make it work, and she found her promotion opportunity later, outside of our team. To be fair, the race for the promotion was probably a close call.

4. THE CORPORATE DIPLOMACY CHALLENGE
"I didn't know who to connect with, how to do it, and what to say..."

With higher-level promotions, there typically comes an increased need to influence key stakeholders indirectly and more skillfully, but how to do this? Who are the key stakeholders, where do I locate them, and should I be using organization charts? Even if I did, how do I reach out to them and make the connection? Nobody wants to come across as awkward by sending a coffee invite to a board member without being clear what they would like to get out of that meeting, should it ever take place.

To make this happen more effectively, proper mapping of key stakeholders needs to be done, as well as a robust engagement plan that addresses key messages and the frequency of those to relevant stakeholders.

This also requires a much more in-depth understanding of identifying critical decision makers, their agendas, as well as building the right support networks and allies. Every interaction counts, particularly at the highest levels in an organization. A wrong first impression is often extremely hard to be reversed and sometimes comes back to bite the executive at crucial moments in their career.

The biggest challenge is often finding critical stakeholders outside of the organization charts. I don't know about you, but as a new leader, most of my executive transition coaching clients aren't able to locate these people on organization charts or by job titles.

It takes many conversations and a structured approach, next to having a "nose" for organizational insights and dynamics to locate these critical and influential stakeholders. Possessing high levels of emotional intelligence is critical here as is the ability to read the (board) room and other interactions among fellow executives.

Sometimes the conversations at the water cooler and short casual conversations from the lift (elevator) to the boardroom can be more revealing than the corporate dashboards and formal corporate information stored in data warehouses. At the time of writing this book, most water cooler conversations have either disappeared or moved to conference calls given the global pandemic.

5. THE INTERNATIONAL MOVE CHALLENGE

"Although I had been a people leader before, I didn't know how to act, behave, or lead..."

I consider myself to be very fortunate to have lived and worked in five countries across two continents. I have been a local employee, on a commuter assignment to another country, on a long-term international assignment, and for some time also on a local plus or a hybrid employment contract.

Each time I moved internationally, I had to think before acting, dive into a new culture, stay curious, and try to make sense of the new environment and how things are said, done, and expected there. This required education, immersion, and embracing the new culture.

Ironically, this was most stark when I moved from Germany to live and work in the German-speaking part of Switzerland. One could wrongly assume things would be pretty similar, if not the same. How wrong and fatal that assumption would be!

To demonstrate this, let me use an example that can be part of anyone's daily routine: when a German or a Swiss executive orders a coffee at the company HQ's cafeteria. The German's order is more of a command, and this manner can come across as a little harsh for the restrained Swiss. Swiss people tend to be careful, polite, and maybe even a little reserved when it comes to communicating. The Swiss love a good subjunctive—could, would, and should are therefore common. When a Swiss employee asks for a coffee at the same cafeteria, she might say, "I would like to have a coffee please." The German employee, on the other hand, orders his coffee with, "I get a coffee!" (Ich bekomme einen Kaffee). Now imagine the same cultural way of expressing oneself during an executive leadership team meeting.

From working with executive transition coaching clients as well as through my own experience, I know how challenging it can be to transition into a new role, and sometimes into a new organization. Having to lead people in an unfamiliar culture, while at the same time moving family and creating a new support network, can also be a real challenge.

No wonder so many international assignments fail due to a lack of cultural adjustment and family-related issues of the expatriate.

Interestingly, when I went back to my home country after living in Western Europe for nineteen years, I had to learn this the hard way. Occasionally, I was reminded culture is very much a living organism, and as a result, things have to be relearned. This is also true in the professional context with the challenges of leading people in a new culture, organization, and industry. Furthermore, the timing of bringing about culture change is as important as how you get it right. We also explored this topic in Chapter 6 when looking at the top ten reasons for executive transition failure.

6. MOVING FROM CORPORATE TO STARTUP OR VICE VERSA

"Who is in charge of this process? Or where does the buck stop here?"

Depending on whether you move from a corporate to a startup company or vice versa, this transition challenge often involves the executive being parachuted by a venture capital (VC) firm. It may also involve a generational gap. Imagine the people and cultural challenges in the following scenario. Two millennial founders grew and led a digital startup company as co-CEOs for a few years before the company was acquired by a large VC firm. Suddenly, a much more experienced baby boomer CEO is in charge, calling the shots, and making key decisions. One can imagine the daily clashes about what is the right strategy going forward, how to execute it, who to hire, etc. The cofounders suddenly find themselves sitting in a corporate board room wearing the corporate shackles and having to explain things and asking for approval of initiatives. The CEO is simply sitting there silently and watching them struggle and burn in front of the management board.

We have now explored six unique challenges. It is important to note, as Michael D. Watkins has also laid out, the above challenges are by no means a complete list of all the possible transition challenges an executive would face throughout their career (Watkins 2019). Hopefully, these provide an overview and a high-level idea of the challenges and first ideas of how to overcome them.

As you can see, many people and cultural challenges await the transitioning executive, and solutions will depend on the context and capabilities of the executive. Ultimately, all of these can be overcome through better support by the executive's organization as well as through the support of an executive transition coach.

In the next chapter, I'll focus on key executive transition challenges that are business and technical.

CHAPTER 9

KEY EXECUTIVE TRANSITION CHALLENGES: BUSINESS & TECHNICAL

———

You have an MBA, an engineering degree, and you're still confused as to what is the next right course of action?

Welcome to the world of business and technical challenges in executive transitions. In the previous chapter, we discussed six executive transition challenges related to people and culture. In this chapter, we continue focusing on some of the most common challenges executives face that are business-related and technical in nature (Watkins 2019).

MOST COMMON TYPES OF EXECUTIVE TRANSITION CHALLENGES

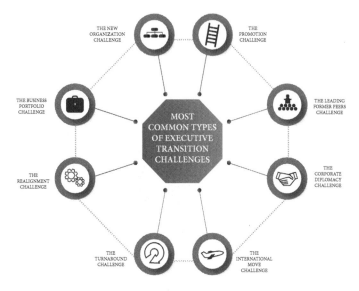

Figure 9.1. Common transition types and the corresponding challenges in *Master Your Next Move* (Watkins 2019).

7. THE TURNAROUND CHALLENGE

"I never worried about this before, but suddenly there was no seat for HR at the table..."

In the past, I was assigned to take over an existing team and work for a business unit that needed a quick and significant turnaround. This business unit was in deep trouble, so I had to figure out rather quickly how to save the team and help them bounce back to avoid a total failure. Through my background, as well as when working with executive HR transition coaching clients, I know this challenge can be a pertinent one in Human Resources. Often the business demands and

HR capabilities don't align. One thinks of the other partner as being too operationally focused, not strategic enough, not commercially focused, or .... (fill in the blank). Aligning these is crucial for the organization to deliver on the people aspect of its business and strategic plan.

8. THE REALIGNMENT CHALLENGE

"Don't you see this ship is sinking?"

This can be a situation where the executive inherits a function or organization that is pretty much in denial about its need for change. Depending on how severe the situation might be, this could lead to a proper turnaround situation. In one instance, a managing director and I were asked to lead the business unit and the Human Resources function that had scored very low globally. Subsequently, I had to turn the HR function around by looking at what was working (very little), what needed to improve, and which people practices had to be newly established so we could support the turnaround of the business. While this was rather painful and laborious, it is hardcore assignments like this that excite me the most!

In our interview, Dr. Hannes Ametsreiter, the CEO of Vodafone Germany and member of the executive committee of Vodafone Group Plc, referred to this turnaround situation:

> *When it was announced I was going to be joining Vodafone in Germany, I received a call from René Obermann, the former CEO of Deutsche Telekom AG, who I knew because I had worked in the telecom industry for*

more than twenty years. He said, "What are you doing, why are you joining Vodafone?" He added, in German, "Die stehen für nichts in Deutschland." So, he said they don't stand for anything in Germany. They have no key positioning and they are losing market share. Why are you going there?

For me it was exactly that: a challenge. I also believed I had the skills to contribute positively to the development of the company. Why? Because I am a marketing expert, and this was a marketing story—how to bring it into growth again, find a good value proposition, find a clear and compelling vision for the company, and then develop it.

I wasn't sure whether it would work, but I made sure everybody had a clear understanding of the challenge ahead. It was a burning platform, and this had not been clear in the teams. So this was something where I clearly understood the hint from René Obermann: There's no value proposition, and there is no differentiation. So, you need to work on differentiation, you need to have a clear profile, Vodafone Germany had lost its profile, its value proposition, and didn't have a clear and compelling vision. So, for me, it was clear I needed to focus on that.

You need to have that critical understanding. What is the one thing you really need to land, and what are the other things that are fine? Having the focus, generating success, and following that vision, I think that's super important, and you need to have the buy-in of your people.

9. THE BUSINESS PORTFOLIO CHALLENGE

"I found myself confused between two very different cultures, organization models, and ways of working in a post-merger integration situation..."

I once had the pleasure of leading the integration of two commercial business units into one. This was not only very exciting, but it also provided a fantastic learning opportunity for me and the respective Managing Directors of the two commercial business units. However, having to deal with the politics on both sides—the multinational parent company that had made the acquisition and the acquired local champion—was not particularly enjoyable. In addition to the many business decisions that had to be made on the future of the merged commercial business unit, and bearing in mind the context of the strategic merger, there were many organizational and cultural issues to overcome.

Plus, as a result of the post-merger integration's To-BE organizational design, we faced a surplus talent situation which required the reduction of a double-digit number of director-level leaders. From my work with executive transition coaching clients, I know how tricky situations like this can be and how one needs to tread lightly. What we decided to do was to involve an external consulting firm to perform executive assessments to get additional data points on who would be the best hire for each role. We also worked actively on a number of cases to find opportunities outside of the consumer business unit but within the wider organization. All of this helped to establish a culture around transparency, fairness, and the best of both worlds on the back end of the merger.

10. THE CROSS-FUNCTIONAL CHALLENGE

"I found myself in Human Resources, drowning in people issues, and nothing seemed to make sense or work..."

Have you ever changed functions and accepted a cross-functional move that was coupled with a promotion or a demotion? Then you know this means you have to deal with two different challenges in one. A cross-functional move is when someone moves from a functional role into a general management role or vice versa. Or alternatively, when someone moves from one function to another.

I had been a successful sales leader and knew all about sales and how to "make it work." Six years later, I found myself in Human Resources and nothing seemed to make sense or work!

My professional career began commercially, where I spent six successful years in business to consumer (B2C) and in business to business (B2B) sales. To be perfectly honest, I never planned to work in the HR function. My perception of HR functions and HR teams back then was that while these were nice colleagues, they lacked customer insights, were too operationally focused, and simply too far removed from the realities of business to make a meaningful impact.

When I interacted with a truly impactful HR business partner for the first time, my view of the HR world changed dramatically. This was a kind of HR "type" I had never experienced before. Her frequent and powerful interactions demonstrated how HR work can be meaningful and make a real impact on the business, customers, and wider stakeholder groups.

I saw for the first time HR can be impactful and, having spent six years in commercial roles, was a real advantage to the HR organization. The fact that I had been a customer of HR for six years helped me enormously to understand what customers actually want from HR and what it feels like to be on "the other side."

So, it became a conscious decision to change my role and shift focus from hardcore sales to Human Resources. Frankly, nobody in HR gave me an early round of applause or a vote of confidence as a result of my commercial background!

I had to perform from day one like any other "assistant HR manager" working for Adidas, the world's most famous three stripes. All it took was for my line manager (Thank you, Danja Frech!) to have faith in my abilities and my learning agility, and I would be successful in an entirely new function.

The upside to that was I didn't have to try hard to demonstrate my commercial skills, nor did I have to struggle to imagine what it would be like to be a customer of HR and how to improve that experience.

The same applies to my executive transition coaching clients who make a cross-functional move (so from a functional role into a general management role or vice versa). There are many unknowns, and it is, therefore, even more critical to work with an experienced executive transition coach to minimize the risk of failure and accelerate the cross-functional transition. In one case, it was a highly established research and development executive who was offered the opportunity to lead the entire business unit, with profit and loss accountability. Suddenly the major focus of their role shifted from being a brilliant scientist and delivering great innovations to spending over sixty percent of their time managing people. This sudden shift can be a huge challenge.

11. THE NEWLY-CREATED-ROLE CHALLENGE

"I found myself for the first time in a global role that had been newly created, and the expectations varied quite widely based on my conversations with different senior stakeholders..."

Have you ever worked in a newly created role in an organization? A role that never existed before and, hence, is created for the very first time? I have when I was hired externally to work for a large multinational in a newly created global role in their corporate headquarters. The first few days felt quite liberating! Then I got my first bruise when one of the members of the HR leadership team felt I had overstepped my boundaries and veered into her area of responsibility. Before I knew it, I had what can be considered "burned fingers."

I believe it is the famous quote from Will Rogers that states, "You never get a second chance to make a first impression."

Well, that was certainly true in my case since our relationship never fully recovered after that. I know how delicate such situations can be. Sometimes these senior positions are created at the highest levels of the organization but left to the incumbent to shape them. Often, they provide the perfect recipe for clashes with roles and responsibilities of more established lines of business and their leaders.

12. THE WINDING-DOWN CHALLENGE
"It must have felt like trying to plug holes in a bucket that is full of water..."

Have you ever had to perform in a role where you had to wind down the entire business operation?

This is one I have not faced myself before. However, a colleague of mine left the organization where we had worked together for many years to join another company in a number one HR capacity. Only a few months in the role, a major and sustained business disruption meant he and the executive committee had to partially sell off some of the assets of the business and wind down the remainder entirely. He was simply unlucky to face this unexpected and unprecedented challenge. Also, from working with many clients, I know how sometimes they deliberately enter into these roles to do what is necessary for that organization.

As we can see, there are many challenges executives can face during their transition that are business and technical in nature. In these two chapters, I have only captured a total of twelve executive transition challenges.

It is quite likely you will face multiple challenges when going through the same transition. My personal advice is you should seek external transition support when you are faced with more than one challenge at the same time. You could very easily face a triple-challenge when you are (1) promoted (2) into a new organization (3) that is facing a business portfolio challenge. One could think of many more challenges executives face when going through their transitions.

In the next chapter, I'll lay out in detail the business case for successful executive transitions.

CHAPTER 10

THE BUSINESS CASE FOR SUCCESSFUL EXECUTIVE TRANSITIONS

It's your first day in a new executive role. You've received your tech toys, software, a functioning email address, access to the intranet, your new employee badge, and even the required access to the board-level floor. Great onboarding, some might think. Not really, I would say. What would please about 99 percent of the employee population in a company is nowhere nearly sufficient for executive-level onboarding.

In this chapter we are going to find out why moving the focus from basic onboarding to proper, successful executive transitions is a no-brainer. Basic onboarding includes things as mentioned above, but an executive transition is a much more aspirational undertaking. Companies need to be doing what it takes to make the new executive a fully functioning and effective member of the executive leadership team as quickly and smoothly as possible.

A study from the Aberdeen Group looked into the onboarding processes of 282 organizations. They found the difference between organizations that get onboarding right and the laggard companies (bottom 30 percent) is significant. Best-in-class companies (top 20 percent) were able to distinguish themselves across key performance criteria (Lombardi 2011):

- 96 percent of first-year employees were retained, as compared to 18 percent of employees at laggard organizations.
- 82 percent of employees hired in the last twelve months met their first performance milestone on time, as compared to 3 percent at laggard organizations.
- 18 percent year-on-year improvement in hiring manager satisfaction, compared to a 1 percent *decrease* among laggard organizations.
- Improvement in customer satisfaction by 12 percent and customer retention by 10 percent, compared to a 2 percent improvement of each at laggard organizations.

The competitive maturity assessment of the same study distilled the common characteristics of the best-in-class organizations, too. They involved a wide range of stakeholders, from individuals to company executives, taking ownership for their role in ensuring the productivity of newly hired employees.

The best-in-class also used a structured and standardized onboarding process that addressed both tactical and strategic elements. They also used metrics to measure and improve the process continuously, as well as partially automated certain elements of onboarding to free up resources to focus on engaging and socializing new employees. An interesting observation is 52 percent of the best-in-class organizations involve their senior ranking executive leaders in the onboarding process, compared to 29 percent of the laggard organizations (Lombardi 2011).

THE RIPPLE EFFECTS

Another study from the Corporate Executive Board (CEB) examines the ripple effect of high-impact leadership transitions. They examined over thirty thousand executive leader transitions, enriched further by hundreds of executive leader interviews. They found the direct reports of a struggling transitioning executive leader on average perform 15 percent worse than those who report to a high-performing one, so a clear performance drag (CEB 2012).

Furthermore, in comparing the likelihood of the direct reports of high-performing versus struggling transitioning leaders to be highly engaged or remain in the organization, they found a statistically significant difference of 20 percent. If we add to this the set of executive peers whose productivity is enhanced because they depend on the executive leader and additional business opportunities that are generated, the ripple effects of executive transitions become truly magnified.

Lastly, CEB's rich database suggests any large organization has seventy senior executives on average. With about 12 percent being replaced annually, this results in eight senior executive transitions each year. Despite this predictable pattern, many organizations approach executive transitions like mergers and acquisitions. We know one of the most commonly identified factors when it comes to failed deals is ineffective post-merger integration. Similarly, most executive transitions fail because of poor "integration" of the leader into the new role in an organization.

The best organizations truly understand the ripple effects (both positive and negative) and orchestrate a structured and externally supported executive transition process. This process would mobilize internal resources and apply innovative tools and systemic approaches to assist the newly appointed executive with a set of high-impact transition activities.

I could stop here and the above would be enough to demonstrate how the best organizations recognize executive transitions occur regularly and must be managed as carefully as other recurring, high-impact business and people processes.

During our interview, Dr. Brian Underhill, CEO of Coach-Source, referred to the importance of reading the culture and building relationships:

> Realizing how important these are and coaches are well suited to help a leader do these things. You can't underestimate the culture of an organization, but it's not always easy to see. Effective coaches are pretty attuned to this and are able to help leaders get a sense of cultural aspects of an organization, where the leader might run into resistance, and the sacred cows.

I tell my clients your first couple of months are data points you should be banking in your head, anything you feel that's a bit odd or different could be some artifact of the culture you're interacting with. You should write them down and remember them because eventually you get deep into the culture, and you stop seeing some of this stuff since you become a part of it. Because you're new, you see things other people can't see as they are already part of it.

I also can't over-highlight how important it is during the first six months or so to build relationships and really spend time getting to know key people by doing one-on-ones and attending team meetings, learning the lay of the land, and figuring out how things work in the new environment.

Significant research has been conducted to evaluate the benefits of successful onboarding and executive transitions. Many studies have focused on benefits related to the leader in transition. However, the benefits are threefold, benefitting at least three distinct groups of stakeholders. Let's take a closer look at them and find out what these benefits are.

BENEFITS FOR THE INDIVIDUAL

A successful transition has proven to reduce the likelihood of derailment by up to 50 percent (Wheeler 2009). A structured and supported executive transition also mitigates key transition challenges and associated risks. In return, enhanced role satisfaction is a clear benefit for the executive leader.

When transitioning follows a structured yet fluid methodology and is supported by an external transition coach (and not a leadership development coach), the likelihood of derailment is significantly reduced. Negative surprises are minimized, and as and when they arise, they are dealt with and de-risked. As a result, several other benefits arise. The most obvious benefit to the executive is the enhanced satisfaction with their new role.

The other benefit that shouldn't go unnoticed is baseline productivity levels are reached in a shorter space of time. This has been measured in many studies and the results are an accelerated transition that is up to 50 percent faster than with the peer group who didn't get the structured transition support.

Genesis Advisers surveyed a sample of executives who received executive transition support, as well as their hiring managers, HR business partners, and the coaches providing the integration support. To measure impact, they asked each group to make estimates of the percentage reduction in time for the executives to become fully effective. The results, summarized below, show the right support for integration can halve the time it takes for newly hired leaders to get up to speed. Given the speed at which business is moving, success in realizing a 50 percent gain for new executive hires would create a very substantial benefit to any organization, particularly at the senior level (Watkins 2017). Other studies by Russell Reynolds Associates and Dai De Meuse & Geddert have come to similar conclusions (Dineen 2021).

I will never forget the above also paid a positive dividend on my work performance and overall well-being. The least obvious benefit is one that is for the long term: through applying a structured framework and by being supported by a specialized executive transition coach, I also learned an enduring skill set that can be applied throughout the rest of my career. Not only did it make me more successful in my role back then, but it also came in handy when I had to transition next. It also positioned me well for enhanced professional career opportunities on the back end of that role, both inside my organization as well as externally.

Lastly, it becomes obvious how successful executive transitions will pay a dividend in an area that has not been mentioned yet: the future trajectory of the executive's career, be it a higher likelihood to be promoted internally or externally after one or more successful transitions. As we can see, there are multiple benefits for the executive and all of the above will ultimately maximize the executive's effectiveness and performance in their new role.

BENEFITS FOR THE ORGANIZATION

While the above-mentioned benefits for the individual are more than enough to understand how valuable successful executive transitions can be, there are more benefits than these when we look at them through the lens of the organization. After all, this chapter is titled "The Business Case for Successful Executive Transitions," and a solid business case usually takes a 360-degree view of the matter.

The most obvious benefit is successful executive transitions reduce the risk of high-stakes placements and potential costs related to mis-hiring. In Chapter 7 we learned mis-hiring at the executive level is highly costly, with an estimate of somewhere between 2.5 to 30 times the salary cost of an executive (Fatemi 2016).

Let's imagine a situation where an organization has just had to announce a surprise departure of their newly hired CEO. Leaving aside the potential reputational damage and the competitive cost that comes when the organization has to work with an interim CEO, there is another undeniable cost that has just been added to the price tag of the new CEO. By creating the perception of being a risky and unsupportive board and organization, prospective CEOs may politely decline the opportunity to even have a conversation with a search firm.

In return, that will most likely affect the "risk premium" that needs to be granted to any incoming CEO and, in a worst-case scenario, impact the quality of available candidates for that role. There is a limit to how long the number two inside an organization, or an ex-board member who has to step down from the board to steer the ship, can continue in that role. Meanwhile, customers are jumping ship, market share is being eaten up by competition, and cultural issues may surface that will take a long time to be tackled, eroding employee engagement levels, innovation, and customer satisfaction.

I have observed this myself firsthand when working in countries in the Middle East that are considered to be hardship locations and, generally speaking, are considered high-risk given the turbulent market dynamics and political landscape. Not only had the executive role been artificially upgraded to make the package more interesting to prospective internal executives, but it also meant the real high potentials were not interested in such roles, so we ended up hiring from the second or third bench of leaders who were technically qualified for the job, but were extremely cautious once in the role and more motivated for the wrong reasons, namely the package.

Corporate Executive Board (CEB) research suggests unsuccessful transitions result in 15 percent lower performance and lower employee engagement, with team members 20 percent more likely to be disengaged or to leave the organization. The flip side of this is 90 percent of leadership teams whose executive leader had a successful transition go on to achieve their three-year performance goals. In those teams, the attrition risk is 13 percent lower than the rest (Keller and Meaney 2018). Decreasing executive attrition directly impacts executive retention in return. Can you begin to imagine the trickle-down effects of this?

Sean Dineen, managing director of Russell Reynolds Associates, referred to this recently during an online panel conversation:

> When you put a structured and thoughtful program in place, the benefits are huge. When you reduce the ramp up time, you kind of break that breakeven point so that it moves forward from six to seven months down to three months. When you look at the broader research on this topic, it leads to two and a half times revenue growth, and two times an increase in profit margin.

So, it's table stakes. If you want to set up a CEO for success, their transition is something you really need to be thinking through carefully (Dineen 2021).

A successful transition also suggests the organization is making better—if not the best—use of the executive's unique talents and potential. It is a strong and clear demonstration of the commitment to the executive and their professional development.

By supporting the executive transition through a structured framework and using the help of an established executive transition coach, organizations increase the chances of creativity, learning, and knowledge sharing too. We can see how this will motivate the executive, their leadership team, and all the other teams and individuals who report to them. Improved relationships between the executive, their leadership team, and the teams reporting to them is likely to break down organizational silos, too.

Furthermore, if part of the mandate of the new executive is to change the organizational culture, then a structured transition supported by an executive transition coach can facilitate the adoption of a new and supportive organizational culture and management style. Also, it helps to reduce organizational anxiety by sending signals of proactive and thoughtful leadership.

Just imagine the scenario where, in quick succession, two CEOs have been pushed out, failed, or quit on their own. How will the increased organizational anxiety levels impact employee engagement levels, customer satisfaction, innovation, and business results?

In summary, the increase in the executive's performance and productivity level will directly impact the organizational performance, productivity, and engagement in return.

BENEFITS FOR THE STAKEHOLDERS

Again, we could stop here as the above-mentioned benefits of successful executive transitions for the individual and the organization are very intriguing and comprehensible. Yet, there are even more benefits to this, when we look at them through the lens of the stakeholders.

The RBL Group, a Human Resources consulting firm, published their findings in "The Leadership Gap," a study with 430 portfolio managers and institutional investors. They found the top three criteria for an investment decision are: how the company performs with 38.5 percent, industry favorableness with 33.1 percent, and quality of leadership with 28.4 percent (Ulrich 2020).

What is particularly interesting is the RBL Group also measured the confidence levels these investors had in their ability to assess the three criteria. The lowest confidence intervals were shown at the quality of leadership with 3.75 or a standard deviation of 0.96 versus 0.58 for performing firms and 0.66 for industry favorableness. That means investors and portfolio managers have the lowest confidence level when it comes to being able to measure the quality of leadership.

Part of what makes the quality of leadership is onboarding executive leaders effectively and minimizing their chances of derailment.

With these findings, we are now able to relate financial investment decisions to companies with their executive transition process.

The study quotes one investor stating, "This is a leading, non-financial indicator, yet all information systems and research services are designed to provide financial metrics. Quality of leadership, culture, and relationships with core stakeholders are critical to understand, but also difficult to gauge. We've spent four years trying to get better in this area."

Now we know investors tend to focus on company performance and industry favorableness, and they have relatively high confidence in the assessments they make in those areas. What is important to note is they also pay attention to the quality of leadership, despite having much lower confidence in how to measure it. So, how can investors better judge the quality of leadership in an organization? The study suggests more rigorous analytical tools to determine the quality of leadership within potential investment opportunities.

On top of this, I propose the investment community will be well served to dive deeper into how top-level executives in a company have churned previously, and what the effectiveness of their executive onboarding process looks like. It is clear if investors had better information about the quality of leadership within a company, they would reduce their risk, increase their confidence, and make more informed investment decisions. In return, the organizations would benefit from more investments at higher confidence intervals, signaling more attraction to medium- and long-term investors.

Another obvious benefit is the combined result of having a high-performing executive, their leadership team, and the organization. It exudes confidence to the management board and to investors. We really shouldn't need research to see how greater alignment of an organizational strategy with cultural execution can increase employee engagement levels and the business performance of an organization.

Successful executive transitions at the very top also provide a platform for thoughtfully engaging external stakeholders. When we look at what the younger generations truly want from their organization, it becomes obvious some of the above are not "nice-to-haves" but indeed "must-haves."

Let's look at the summary overview of the key differences in outcomes between basic onboarding and successful executive transitions.

THE BUSINESS CASE FOR SUCCESSFUL EXECUTIVE TRANSITIONS

BASIC ONBOARDING		SUCCESSFUL TRANSITIONS
67% of company strategies fail due to poor execution	▶	90% likelihood that executive & team meet 3-Y performance goals
Flat or declining revenue growth & profit margin	▶	2.5x Revenue Growth 2x increase in Profit Margins
40% of executive hires are pushed out, fail or quit	▶	50% lower attrition risk & derailment risk reduced by 50%+
Replacement cost of an executive 2.5-30X salary	▶	Significant opportunity cost saved
Ramp up time external hires 6-9 Mo. Ramp up time internal hires 3-9 Mo.	▶	50% reduced ramp up time

SPECIALIZED EXECUTIVE TRANSITION COACH

Figure 10.1. The business case for successful executive transitions: Moving from basic onboarding to successful transitions. Self-created table based on various studies from Corporate Executive Board, *Harvard Business Review*, and Russell Reynolds Associates (Carucci 2017; Keller and Meaney 2018; Fatemi 2016; Nawaz 2017; Wheeler 2009; Masters 2009).

By now the business case for successful executive transitions should be clear and compelling. In the next chapter, I will outline some key interventions for successful executive transitions.

CHAPTER 11

KEY INTERVENTIONS FOR SUCCESSFUL EXECUTIVE TRANSITIONS

An executive transition is one of the most delicate undertakings for any executive and their organization. There are existing onboarding books such as *The First 90 Days* or *The New Leader's 100-Day Action Plan*. Both books are useful for manager onboarding (Watkins 2003; Bradt et al. 2011).

In Chapter 2, we learned while both models from Watkins and Bradt have their merits and can be valuable, a 90–120 day focus isn't sufficient to propel an executive into a new leadership role and organization, ensuring a successful transition.

Let's take a look at some key interventions for successful executive transitions. For me, this is the equivalent of a diamond mine where we explore key interventions that make executive transitions more successful, reduce the time to productivity, and de-risk them significantly. The interventions are comparable to diamonds in the rough, and once cut and polished, their true value emerges. Speaking of diamonds, we will learn more about the Double Diamond Framework© of Executive Transitions in Chapters 12 and 13.

INTERVENTION #1: EXECUTIVE TRANSITION COACHING, TARGETING THE TOP 3 GROUPED REASONS FOR FAILURE

The first intervention may not be obvious. You may remember in Chapter 6 we looked at the top ten reasons for executive transition failure. I also painted the picture of the top three grouped reasons for failure. As expected, these are neither technical nor functional. So, hiring your next Chief Human Resources Officer and finding out they are not any good when it comes to people management is rare.

As a reminder, the top three grouped reasons for executive transition failure are: culture, people, and politics.

TOP 3 GROUPED REASONS FOR EXECUTIVE FAILURES

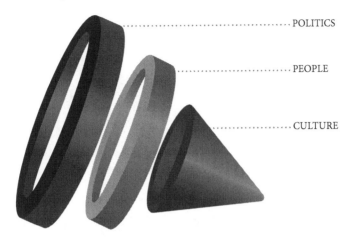

.... POLITICS

.... PEOPLE

.... CULTURE

Figure 11.1. Top three grouped reasons for executive transition failures. Created by Navid Nazemian Executive Coaching in 2021.

All of these are soft-skills-related challenges or opportunities, depending on how you look at them. When we look at the key focus and expertise of typical executive transition coaches highlighted in Chapter 4, it becomes obvious they can support the executive unreservedly in these three areas. Not only will they utilize some of the toolkits and frameworks to be proactive, but they are also equipped to identify gaps in competencies and behaviors and provide strategic and proven mitigation strategies. Some of these toolkits include a reliable and verified assessment (such as the HOGAN Leads Series), an executive assimilation process, a thorough and robust stakeholder engagement plan, and an executive elevator pitch, preparing the executive for crucial conversations, and more.

The above is arguably the simplest intervention to maximize your chances of success and speed up your time to productivity.

If you were to ignore all other advice in this book, simply go ahead and equip your transitioning executive with a qualified executive transition coach.

INTERVENTION #2: THE SUCCESSFUL INTERIM EXECUTIVE MODEL

The second intervention is from a related industry, namely that of interim management. Why is this relevant, you may ask? Think of interim executives as serial "transitioners." Given that they transition with a high level of effectiveness in often varied circumstances, interim executives typically must complete their transition and flip into meaningful action in less than ten days (Fishman 2008).

The following research is based on an interview I conducted with Anton Fishman for this book. Anton is an organizational consultant and senior partner to many firms. He was also a senior partner at one of the largest interim management firms in Europe called Alium Partners, now firming as Boyden. He found there are structured ways of orientating and onboarding such leaders. As Anton explained:

I embarked on a research project into interim executive transitions. I interviewed just under two dozen senior people in a variety of different roles, from interim chief executives, company doctors who were turnaround experts, to interim HR directors, finance directors, and the like. My investigation was explicitly this: "Tell me how, as you enter into your new organization, you ensure your interim assignment is successful."

I soon learned something which struck me as fascinating. A few people, were very planful in what they did. For them it was an explicit process. However, for most interims interviewed this was implicit; they just went in and they transitioned successfully. What was deeply fascinating though was as the many stories of onboarding unfolded, it was as if everyone had read the same textbook. They all described the same incremental process, the same structured progression from relationship building, fact finding, organizational diagnosis through to action planning, re-contracting, and early delivery of quick wins while laying the foundations for long-term impact and a legacy of improved capability to sustain the performance improvements long after they departed.

Anton kindly shared an interesting model with me that I would like to share with you too.

He found that, remarkably, interim executives manage their transition in a consistent and structured way as well as at an extraordinary pace. So, while executives are often granted about 90–120 days by their organization to manage their transition and prepare for appropriate action, interim executives complete their transition and flip into meaningful action in *less than ten days*. One of the reasons is they use their time effectively and systematically.

The above approach truly differentiates the top 20 percent highest performing interim executives from the rest. They were able to outperform customer expectations, irrespective of the assignment, organization size, or industry. Once the interim executive has been appointed, they look at their set of agreed objectives and reflect on the reasons why they have been brought into the business.

They then go on a quick fact-finding mission and start learning about the business. Again, the "First 90 Days" formulae don't apply here, given they may only have ninety days in total (Watkins 2003)! They then start to engage key people who are relevant to their assignment and mission. This is quickly followed by building quick and effective relationships with key people. These four actions ensure they establish their credibility early on.

We're now looking at day two or three, and the wise interim executive has already established some key facts, learned about the business, spoken with key people, and started to build relationships. Do you sense how powerful this approach is?

Now they get into diagnosing the issue at hand, which is the reason why they were brought in to help. They go deeper to find some of the underlying root causes. Very swiftly, they then scope out and answer questions around how to tackle the issue, where to attack, where to be gentle, what resources are required, what needs to be done by when, and so on. All of these answers help to clarify the way ahead.

Given interim executives are typically paid a daily rate, they are costly resources to have. The wise interim executives are cognizant of this and they are aware they don't have much time to get caught up in analysis paralysis.

Ensuring the issue is tackled effectively, while identifying and realizing visible first quick wins, is crucial. What's ironic is the study found oftentimes the interim executives have to go back to their sponsor to renegotiate their initial objectives. This is because the reasons they were brought in may be related to something completely different in the organization.

Once that is done, the last step is to move into swift and determined action.

The study also identified qualities that enable interim executives to successfully manage their transition:

THE SUCCESSFUL INTERIM MANAGEMENT MODEL

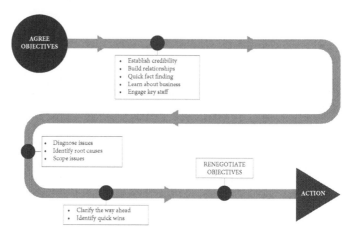

Figure 11.2. The successful interim management model.
"How Interim Managers transition into new roles—A behavioral investigation of successful entry strategies," First International Conference for Research into Interim Management, Cass Business School, November 2008, Alium Partners Limited. Reproduced with permission from Anton Fishman (Fishman 2021).

INTERVENTION #3: CEO TRANSITION CHECKLIST

McKinsey & Company suggests executives think about mounting a transition in two equal steps (Keller and Meaney 2018). First, take stock, and then take action across the following five dimensions: your business or function, culture, team, yourself, and other stakeholders.

Our third intervention looks at what the former managing director of McKinsey, Sir Ian Edward Lamert Davis, wrote in a published letter to an incoming CEO. Therein he suggests the following steps be taken during the upcoming transition (Davis 2010).

I've taken the essence of that letter and created a list of the top ten items you can use as a checklist. Some of these will be familiar to you by now as we have already touched upon them. Broadly speaking, they can be applied by other executives who are not necessarily CEOs.

CEO TRANSITION—A CHECKLIST	
1. Have I reflected on the context of my transition not just from my own perspective, but from that of all key stakeholders?	☐
2. Have I established in my own mind the time frame and intended outcomes of my leadership transition?	☐
3. Have I established my initial set of priorities with a full understanding of what others expect of me?	☐
4. How will I control my agenda and allocate my time?	☐
5. Have I developed a clear process and time frame for selecting my top team?	☐
6. Have I committed sufficiently to building a relationship with my chairman and the board of directors?	☐
7. Do I have a mechanism for building the necessary support office and infrastructure?	☐
8. Have I thought through my communications plan—internal and external?	☐
9. Do I have a mechanism for getting balanced feedback and information?	☐
10. Have I established appropriate personal ground rules?	☐

Figure 11.3. The CEO transition in form of a checklist. Image has been recreated from the article, "Letter to a Newly Appointed CEO" in 2021 (Davis 2010).

INTERVENTION #4: THE EXTENT OF ONBOARDING SUPPORT

A joint Genesis and Egon Zehnder study looked at the extent of support executives get when new in the role (Triantogiannis, Watkins, and Byford 2017). Here it becomes clear that typically the executive's direct reports (30 percent) and line manager (25 percent) are most supportive while the executive's peers (12 percent), when asked for support of the onboarding, aren't very supportive. An interesting observation is the role of the HR business partner (16 percent). They can be either very helpful or not helpful at all.

I've seen many executive coaching clients making that same mistake: they assume the critical stakeholder groups are equally relevant and important for their onboarding. The reality, according to the research, is that it isn't true (Triantogiannis, Watkins, and Byford 2017).

The most important stakeholders are the direct reports and the line manager. Over and above that, the HR partner (likely the CHRO or the HR director supporting the executive) is another critical stakeholder. Which one have you inherited, though, the helpful one or the detractor? It is ultimately determined by the quality of the HR leader and their genuine intent to support the transitioning executive. I think the biggest surprise of the study is the fact that the peers are not a key stakeholder group to support the leader with their onboarding.

To be clear, the study isn't suggesting ignoring your peers. What it indicates is peers are most likely too busy to worry about your onboarding and it really isn't *their* key priority (Triantogiannis, Watkins, and Byford 2017). The wise executive bears that in mind when transitioning.

INTERVENTION #5: DIFFERENCE BETWEEN SMOOTH AND DIFFICULT TRANSITIONS

A recent study by Development Dimensions International (DDI) found there are key differences between senior leaders who mentioned they went through a "smooth transition" ("is there really such a thing as a smooth transition?" some of us may be thinking by now) and "difficult transition" (sounds about right). The differences mostly relate to the executive's organization and how helpful they were in supporting the transitioning executive (Development Dimensions International 2021).

DDI identified six interventions that stand between smooth and difficult transitions:

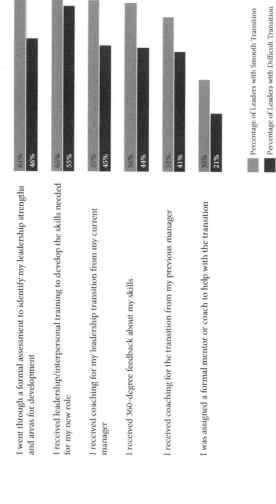

HOW ORGANIZATIONAL SUPPORT IMPACT EXECUTIVE TRANSITIONS

I went through a formal assessment to identify my leadership strengths and areas for development — 61% / 46%

I received leadership/interpersonal training to develop the skills needed for my new role — 65% / 55%

I received coaching for my leadership transition from my current manager — 57% / 45%

I received 360-degree feedback about my skills — 56% / 44%

I received coaching for the transition from my previous manager — 52% / 41%

I was assigned a formal mentor or coach to help with the transition — 30% / 21%

Percentage of Leaders with Smooth Transition
Percentage of Leaders with Difficult Transition

Figure 11.4. How organizational support impacts executive transitions. In "Leadership Transitions Report 2021," Global Leadership Forecast Series. Reproduced with permission from Development Dimensions International, 2021.

First, providing the executive with a formal assessment to identify their leadership strengths and areas for development. Over the years, I have used an assessment tool called HOGAN Leads Series to establish that. However, there are many more tools out there such as the Leadership Versatility Index (LVI) or the Leadership Circle Profile. Ultimately it is a matter of whether the client organization has an established tool they value and use, or if the coach and executive get to select the best possible tool.

Second, receive leadership or interpersonal training to develop the skills required in the new executive role. At the top end, this will be less of a classroom training and more of working one-on-one with an executive transition coach.

Third, receiving coaching and support from the executive's *current* line manager. I would like to point out the term "coaching" is used widely in the management world. So, can a line manager ever be a true coach (in the real sense of the word and practice) to their direct reports? Some would argue it is indeed possible; however, multiple hurdles need to be overcome. David Clutterbuck, a famous team coach, has outlined in a 2012 blog post, citing an original study of Stephen Ferrar from Oxford Brookes University, the behaviors and habits that could get in the way:

- The tendency for managers and direct reports to fall into "parent-child" roles in any conversation.
- The sense both parties may have hidden agendas (for example, on the manager's part about their plans to reorganize the team and on the employee's part about how long they intend to stay with the company).

- The conflict between the employee's desire for some things to remain confidential and the manager's accountability for the welfare and performance of the team as a whole.
- The conflict between pressure to deliver short-term task objectives and the longer-term development needs of team members.
- Groupthink. People who work together tend to adopt the same filters on the world around them and have the same blind spots. Paradoxically, the better the relationship between line manager and learner, the more likely this is to be the case.
- Inequality in who gets coaching (Clutterbuck 2012). Time pressures often mean the manager concentrates coaching on particular individuals or subgroups of the team. This could be because they have either bigger performance problems or greater potential. If the former, people often resent being "picked on;" if the latter, other people resent being left out. In such situations, the line manager as a coach can't win!

For me, the two most obvious challenges are the lack of impartiality and established lines of reporting. So, in order to make this particular intervention work, the concept of manager as a coach essentially means line managers should make more use of tools such as open-ended questions (vs. providing answers) or listening (vs. speaking), etc.

Fourth, undergoing a 360-degree assessment. It is obvious how having a starting point and an established baseline in the form of a 360-feedback tool can be beneficial to the leader. It may be equally beneficial to apply the same tool at the end of year one and before concluding the coaching engagement.

Fifth, receiving coaching and support from the executive's *previous* line manager. As outlined during the fifth intervention above, this is possible. However, the above-mentioned hurdles have to be overcome to make this work effectively.

Last, get assigned a formal mentor or an executive transition coach. This is a fascinating finding since the same study showed there is a 13 percent to 22 percent gap between female executives and their male counterparts. In particular, being assigned a formal mentor or coach to support the onboarding has the largest gap of 22 percent between female and male respondents. Male executives seem to get more support. One can only guess why there would be different treatments based on gender. While this is speculative, I have made the following observations over the years (Development Dimensions International 2021).

First, the issue begins with the organization not offering this support in a structured and consistent way, e.g., if mentoring or executive coaching support is built into the executive onboarding process, then there shouldn't be a gender difference of who gets it and who doesn't.

Second, and for the lack of a better phrase, let's call it "excessive readiness." I have observed male executives more generally to be putting themselves forward to be considered for executive positions more readily. I have also found many of them to be more demanding than their female counterparts. For example, putting themselves forward for executive positions regardless of whether the hiring manager and HR share the same view or not, negotiating their new package, or making demands that are not necessarily covered by the people policies of the organization, such as the corner office, a second personal assistant, a chauffeur, etc.

This isn't a discussion about entitlement; these are merely my personal observations from the corporate world.

INTERVENTION #6: START BEFORE YOU ONBOARD

In the 2011 publication *Before Onboarding: How to Integrate New Leaders for Quick and Sustained Results*, the title of Michael Burroughs' book, gives it away.

Burroughs goes further to recommend that:

> *Executive Coaching has proved to be the most effective developmental vehicle for executives. An experienced executive coach can serve a larger role than a leadership or management developer. A good executive coach can also serve as a sounding board and guide during leader transitions. The one-on-one private nature of the coaching process works especially well in this role. The addition of an executive coach at the end of a new leader integration process can help ensure that the new leader continues to advance in the right direction once on board (Burroughs 2011).*

INTERVENTION #7: ONBOARDING ISN'T ENOUGH

In 2017, Watkins subsequently came up with a new framework to assess an organization on its commitment to:

- *basic orientation* (signing up new hires and explaining roles and organizational structure)
- *active assimilation* (making modest efforts to help people understand organizational culture and politics), and
- *accelerated integration* (investing resources in bringing people up to speed quickly).

The research also suggests custom-designed experiences are key to success. Furthermore, he identified the following five key tasks for transitioning leaders: 1. Assume operational leadership, 2. Take charge of the team, 3. Align with stakeholders, 4. Engage with the culture, and 5. Define strategic intent (Triantogiannis, Watkins, and Byford 2017).

In the next chapter, I'll introduce you to the Double Diamond Framework© of Executive Transitions.

CHAPTER 12

INTRODUCTION TO THE DOUBLE DIAMOND FRAMEWORK© OF EXECUTIVE TRANSITIONS

What makes an outstanding diamond?

Chances are you have heard of the five Cs of outstanding diamonds. The quality and value of diamonds are usually judged on five fundamental criteria known also as the "five Cs," which are:

1. Carat-Weight
2. Color
3. Clarity
4. Cut
5. Certification

In this chapter, we're going to the heart of this book, and I'm delighted to introduce you to the Double Diamond Framework© of Executive Transitions.

This framework aims to capture pretty much everything that has been covered thus far in the previous chapters. Metaphorically speaking, we will go right into the heart of the diamond mine. Arguably, no diamond is ever complete or perfect when it is found. Bearing that in mind, I have aimed to reflect the key essence of my mission in this framework: to bend executive transitions *away* from pure luck and failures *toward* the masterful and successfully crafted.

This book is my life's work: supporting people to grow beyond what they imagined possible.

In the case of the Double Diamond Framework©, we will be using a different set of five Cs that are crucial elements for the overall success (quality) of executive transitions. These are:

1. Context (arguably the most important C of all, the circumstances of the organization, competition, landscape, government, and society)
2. Culture (organization, leadership, values)
3. Commitment (what is the organization committed to achieving for its customers, clients, and society?)
4. Circles (of influence, power, and informal decision-making)
5. Confidence (levels of employee engagement and leadership DNA)

THE DOUBLE DIAMOND FRAMEWORK© OF EXECUTIVE TRANSITIONS

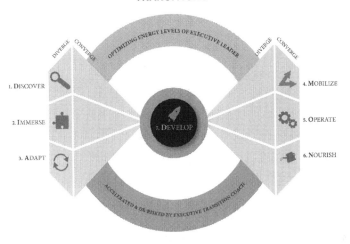

Figure 12.1. The Double Diamond Framework© of Executive Transitions by Navid Nazemian Executive Coaching (Nazemian 2021).

ADVANTAGES OF THE FRAMEWORK

The following describes the advantages associated with applying this structured and repeatable process framework, which offers a tailored approach that enables high executive performance during career transitions:

- Compress and fast track the executive leader's time to productivity.
- Avoid costly, avoidable, and potentially career-limiting blunders.
- Maximize the leadership team's productivity and improve the probability of hitting multi-year performance goals.
- Accelerate executive leadership team cohesiveness.

- Rapidly gain personal and professional credibility with key stakeholders, key customers, major suppliers, trustees, and board members to build a political base and gain commitment.
- Make the executive leader's transition as efficient as possible by laying the foundations for sustained improvement.
- Sustain the newly appointed executive's early successes over the longer term.

Let's take a quick look at the model first before I explain the seven phases that make up the word **DIAMOND**. These are:

1. **Discover**
2. **Immerse**
3. **Adapt**
4. **Mobilize**
5. **Operate**
6. **Nourish**
7. **Develop**

Looking at the cut diamonds from the side, we can see the shapes suggesting the executive will be diverging and converging at different stages throughout their transition. The concept of divergence and convergence isn't new. I took the inspiration from author and podcast host David Perell. In the divergence phase, you playfully explore new ideas, and in the convergence phase, you shift into a state of focus where you simplify your ideas so you can put them into action. As Perell puts it, first collect the dots, then connect them (@ david_perell March 10, 2021). Let's look at the two modes and see how they apply to executive transitions.

DIVERGENCE OR COLLECTING THE DOTS

During divergence, the attitude of the transitioning leader is playful, and activities center on collecting ideas and information. Their mindset is to overcome uncertainties. Their approach during this period is one of exploration and serendipity. The executive is driven by intuition with their focus on many things, such as culture, people, processes, and more. The mindset during divergence is that of an explorer, with the key factor being the constant firing of signals in the executive's brain. We can see how this would predominantly be the case during the minus 90 to the first 90 days or so after starting a new role. This is the "grace period" for the executive, where potentially more time is spent collecting the dots than connecting them. This being said, we also need to remember divergence and convergence can happen in subsequent orders but don't necessarily have to follow one another.

CONVERGENCE OR CONNECTING THE DOTS

During convergence, the transitioning executive's attitude is more focused, and their activities are about refining ideas, rather than collecting them. Their mindset is to look out for certainty, and the approach has shifted from exploring to unearthing with the principle being more about predictability. During convergence, the executive is likely to be driven by goals and objectives and their focus will be on only a few key critical deliverables. Their mindset has shifted from that of an explorer to one that is focused on getting things done. The key factor during convergence is compression.

We must note the seven individual phases of the overall framework are movable and not necessarily fixed. This is important as the Double Diamond Framework© isn't necessarily a step-by-step process, although it certainly can be. It is more iterative and can be looked at as waves that sometimes overlap. Think of the diamond that's kept under light, how flashes of light can also overlap. What is also true is sometimes an entire phase is being skipped, either deliberately or because there simply is no time left for the executive to attend to it.

We can also see two half circles connecting the diamonds. One is the support provided by an experienced executive transition coach, helping the executive to accelerate time to productivity and at the same time de-risk their transition.

The other one reminds us that executive transitions are indeed highly stressful and often energy-depleting. As a result, the executive in transition must ensure they build up and optimize the levels of intent, focus, and energy to endure and, some would say, survive and thrive.

I have certainly often felt that way. In particular, I have found changing industries can be somewhat challenging at the beginning. Moving from retail to sporting goods felt like a natural transition for me, albeit the cross-functional move made it a real challenge. Then moving from sporting goods to commercial finance was certainly very different. From there, I moved to fast-moving consumer goods (FMCG) and was surprised by the simplicity of the business model and the high turnover of product innovations, and the fast pace of the industry.

Moving to pharmaceuticals was definitely a huge challenge for me, particularly the nature of a pharmaceutical company and the distinct ways in which decisions were made at that Swiss giant. From there, moving to a telecommunications company that had high tech ambitions was a real killer. The pace and magnitude of change and transformation were at a whole different level, even when I compare it to my FMCG time.

STRESS LEVELS MEASURED BY SENIORITY

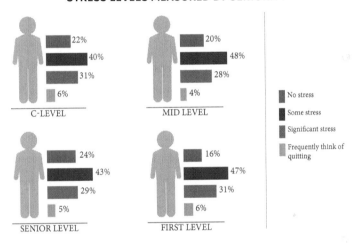

Figure 12.2. Stress levels measured by seniority. In "Leadership Transitions Report 2021," Global Leadership Forecast Series. Reproduced with permission from Development Dimensions International (Development Dimensions International 2021).

The point here is executive transitions are more like a marathon, not a sprint, but the avid runner knows there are many sprints involved to train up to a marathon level. Would you go and register for the next marathon in your city? If you are not a seasoned runner, that concept might sound like a foolish idea to you. Yet, many executives go through their first or second transition without any guidance or experienced support and simply aim to wing it. This, in turn, leads to the 40 percent failure rate of executive transitions during the first eighteen months.

OPTIMIZING ENERGY LEVELS OF THE EXECUTIVE LEADER

During a webinar, Sean Dineen, managing director of Russell Reynolds Associates, spoke about the importance of energy levels required during executive transitions:

> When you look at some of the research around leadership transitions, it is up there as one of the most stressful things somebody can deal with in their life, along with divorce and health issues. So, don't underestimate the tremendous amount of stress the transition is going to put on your CEO, and make sure a support structure is in place, both instrumental advice as well as emotional support.

ENERGY MATTERS MORE THAN TIME

In a ground-breaking article published by *Harvard Business Review* (*HBR*) in 2007, the authors Schwartz and McCarthy provided the evidence and data to demonstrate why energy matters more than time to get things done. The article rightly referred to the increasing demands of leaders in the workplace and how most of them are trying to cope by adding more hours to the working day (as mentioned in Chapter 3 where I highlighted how corporate life for an executive has become exponentially more challenged). Most executives seem to take for granted what exactly fuels their ability to work, namely their energy. The authors argue while time is a finite resource, the same can't be said about energy levels as it can be replenished. However, that would require a systematic expansion and renewed care.

Adding more and more hours to the working day ultimately leads to more burnout. Let's disregard the increase in burn-out rate in 2020–2021 that may in part be due to the global COVID-19 pandemic. However, pre-pandemic research shows us how the level of "clinical exhaustion" has risen globally, particularly in developed nations.

THE EXAMPLE OF SWEDEN
Let's look at one of the most worker-friendly countries in the world: Sweden. It has seen a steep increase in burnout between 2013 and 2019 (Savage 2019). The working conditions are among some of the best in the world for employees. Less than 1 percent of Swedes work fifty hours per week or more. Contrast this with a Gallup report from 2014 that estimated the *average* full-time worker in the United States works forty-seven hours a week, one of the highest figures in the world, and significantly higher than the rates in Western Europe where the Working Time Directive gives employees in the European Union the right to work no more than forty-eight hours a week. In practice, employees in some countries, like Germany and Sweden, work closer to thirty-five hours a week according to Sir Cary Cooper, CBE, an American-born professor at Manchester Business School in the United Kingdom.

Swedish citizens are furthermore guaranteed a five-week long holiday and there is a very strongly established culture of flexible working, next to having one of the most generous parental leave and subsidized childcare policies in the world. And this is universally true for the Nordic countries in Europe. I was reminded of this when I was on a business trip to Denmark, and after a meeting with the general manager who finished at 16:30, she excused herself as she needed to pick up her children from school before heading home. That same night, she was on a conference call with me and our colleagues who were based in San Francisco.

In 2018, "clinical exhaustion" was the most common reason for Swedes to be off work, accounting for more than 20 percent of sickness benefit cases across all age groups. Even among young workers who arguably enter the workforce with fresh energy levels, cases were up by 144 percent for twenty-five to twenty-nine-year-olds since 2013. While the rise has affected both genders, women were more likely to be off sick due to exhaustion than their male counterparts. The study found women spend more time on household chores, feel more pressured to work out, and achieve things in their spare time, irrespective of whether they have children or not, next to some role-related differences.

This is the second time we have uncovered how executive transitions can be more challenging for female executive leaders than their male counterparts. In Chapter 7, I outlined the other reason: a lower level of executive transition support for female executives compared to their male counterparts even when working for the same organization.

THE ENERGY PROJECT'S FRAMEWORK

We can see how it would make sense to revisit the energy study published in *HBR*, mentioned earlier in this chapter. The authors suggest a framework that focuses on rituals that build energy in the four key dimensions. These are the **body, emotions, mind,** and **spirit,** and they are the wellsprings of energy that can be systematically expanded and renewed.

While I won't be covering the findings of the energy project in full, let's take a quick dive into activities that nurture energy in each of the four key dimensions. I have further enriched these with some practical examples of how I embed these myself.

Body: Harnessing our body's ultradian rhythms by taking sporadic pauses will restore physical energy. When working in the company office, I make it a habit to go and get a cup of water every hour or so instead of bringing a water flask that would avoid my getting away from my desk. Every day I would go out to get lunch instead of having a quick sandwich at my desk, even if it is a twenty- or thirty-minute break. Now and then I'd go for a walking meeting with a colleague, weather and circumstances permitting, instead of sitting in a meeting room or board room.

Emotions: Each time we face adversity, rejecting the role of a victim and instead viewing events through a hopeful lens will defuse negative emotions that can be energy-depleting.

Mind: Avoiding the constant distractions technology has introduced into our daily lives significantly upsurges mental energy. Working as a corporate executive myself, I have made it a habit to permanently switch off email notifications, collaboration tool notifications, and those in professional network tools to concentrate more effectively.

Spirit: When we participate in activities that give us a sense of meaning and purpose, it boosts our energy. For me, this is the meditation practice I picked up back in 2014 as an "experimental homework" and have kept since then.

Rudi Kindts, ex-CHRO and now executive coach, shared the following insights during our interview:

> *A model that helped me enormously in coaching through transitions is the resilience model with three elements in it. The first element is agency, so working on energy. Transitioning often is like bouncing back, but it takes energy, too, because there's euphoria and excitement. If there's no euphoria and no excitement when you arrive, something is wrong. You're unlikely to survive.*
>
> *The second element is survival. That means a lot of energy and a lot of learning. So, one should almost go beyond coping because that takes too much energy, and I have been definitely in survival mode previously. But I am also very resilient. That's my pitfall. Because I can go on, and even when I go home, I just go on, and go on. While I've never had a breakdown or a burnout, I have indeed spilled a lot of energy. The third element is pacing. How do you pace? How do you prioritize? What do you value? Using this resilience model has changed everything for me.*

VALIDITY OF THE MODEL

From a public relations perspective, Leslie Gaines-Ross of Burson-Marsteller applied the stages of John Gabarro's model to the transition of new CEOs and their processes of building great reputations (Gaines-Ross 2002: Gabarro 1987). She found Wall Street analysts, investors, and other key external and internal stakeholders typically gave the CEO about five quarters before the CEO was expected to present his or her selected executive leadership team and a definitive action plan to implement changes to improve the performance of the business. This research is somewhat dated, and when looking at the same through today's lens for pressured CEOs, three to four quarters seems more realistic. For these types of transitions, most of my executive transition coaching assignments have been consistent engagements lasting for twelve months or four quarters.

Like all well-proven business models, the Double Diamond Framework© of Executive Transitions demonstrates robust convergent validity. Convergent validity is indicated when similar results and conclusions are realized by otherwise independent parties testing a similar model. Try applying this model to your own executive leadership experiences. Think of your career and/or the many leaders you might have helped to onboard at the top of the house.

Before we dive deeper into the Double Diamond Framework© of Executive Transitions in the next chapter, let me also give you an idea about some of the tools that are linked to the different phases of the framework. I won't be covering these in this book. However, executives often ask me during our coaching chemistry conversation (where we speak to find out whether working together is the right fit for both of us) what kind of tools and frameworks I use in my practice. So, here's a sneak peek:

SAMPLE OF TOOLS

- **Executive's Life Career Journey Interview**: Establish key events in executive's life and some of the early childhood messages that may have shaped their mental model and ways of being.
- **Executive Values Exercise**: Identify personal values, understand them more deeply, and align with executive career and supporting actions.
- **Executive Career Drivers Assessment**: Assess underlying career drivers and use them to assess against executive career opportunities.
- **HOGAN Leadership Forecast Series Assessment**: Hogan Personality Inventory (HPI) assesses your "normal" personality as it relates to everyday job performance. Hogan Development Survey (HDS) assesses behaviors that can lead to executive derailment. Motives, Values, Preferences Inventory (MVPI) are the values and preferences that motivate you and drive your behavior (Hogan Assessments 2015).
- **Executive Transition Assessment**: Assess upcoming executive transition challenges and where the executive should plan for and focus accordingly.
- **Executive Elevator Pitch Toolkit**: Craft, align, and pitch key messages to critical stakeholders in the safe environment of working with the executive transition coach.
- **Executive Onboarding Interview Questions**: Helps you fine-tune questions aimed at various stakeholder groups

to gain meaningful insights regarding context, the organization, the industry, and fundamental drivers, products, and services.

- **Confidential Executive 360 Interviews:** Get to know your key stakeholders and what they expect from you in the new role and which themes emerge.
- **New Executive Assimilation Toolkit:** Get to know your leadership team, start setting performance expectations, understand leadership team dynamics, establish ways of working, and allow the team to get to know you.
- **Stakeholder Engagement Toolkit:** Map key stakeholders and establish key messages, accountabilities, and the frequency and channels of interaction with them. Establish key priorities with critical stakeholders and eliminate conflicting and ambiguous priorities early on.
- **Executive Legacy IKIGAI Toolkit:** Applying this toolkit helps you to orient toward a more purposeful life, providing a sense of fulfillment and meaning (Gaines 2021).
- **The One Pager of Truth:** Using Dr. BJ Fogg'S Behavior Grid to enable you to receive actionable and condensed insights that are triangulated from the HOGAN assessments, the 360 feedback, as well as the four human domains intake (Fogg 2018).
- **Executive Leader's Last 90–120 Days Toolkit:** Helping you plan your last 90–120 days and successfully transition out of your executive role.

In the next chapter, I'll walk you through the seven phases of the Double Diamond Framework© of Executive Transitions in full detail.

CHAPTER 13

THE DOUBLE DIAMOND© FRAMEWORK OF EXECUTIVE TRANSITIONS

———

In the previous chapter, the Double Diamond Framework© of Executive Transitions was introduced. Let's now deep dive into each phase of the framework and look at typical challenges and derailers. Note all phases are equally important and interdependent.

THE DOUBLE DIAMOND FRAMEWORK© OF EXECUTIVE TRANSITIONS

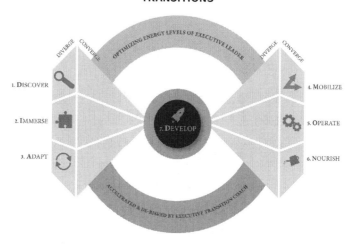

Figure 13.1. The Double Diamond Framework© of Executive Transitions by Navid Nazemian Executive Coaching (Nazemian 2021).

1. DISCOVER

This is the phase often referred to as before onboarding, pre-boarding, or before the starting line. The timing is somewhere between ninety days before, up until day one of starting in the new role. The key tasks for you as the onboarding executive at this phase are to understand the business and its context, establish your credibility, and start to leverage your (new or existing) network and relationships. For some, this also involves learning about the dynamics and value chain of a new industry. If you are an executive who has been internally hired or promoted, you may have a little head start here.

Typical documents to be studied at this phase are annual reports, strategy presentations, investor roadshow presentations, capital market day documents, and web recordings that are often offered on a company's investor relation website, employee engagement surveys, new team related documentation such as talent profiles, performance, and potential ratings, and more. As an incoming executive, you must ensure you understand the shareholder structure, organizational culture, and the prevailing leadership style of your (new) organization. Depending on the nature of the role, this may also require a deep dive into a business unit/line of business, a country presence, or an entire cluster of countries and region(s).

The above reading and studying are further enhanced by conversations with crucial stakeholders. As we learned in the previous chapter, your line manager and direct reports are critical stakeholders to your onboarding success. There are other stakeholders such as Human Resources, your peers, and the board that can also be insightful conversation partners, too.

At an online panel discussion moderated by Russell Reynolds Associates in December 2020, Tina St. Leger, CHRO of GW Pharmaceuticals, described her pre-boarding experience as follows:

> I was never worried about asking too many questions beforehand. Presentations, briefings, and anything I could get hold of, any data beforehand, helped to start to shape my understanding of the organization.

> I did have a mentor about a year before, and as I was thinking about my first CHRO role, I remember her

saying to me two things. One was write everything down, and secondly, don't stop asking questions at the beginning. Write everything down because what you notice on day one might be different today, on day ten, and then on day seventy-two, and so on. So, I wrote everything down, and I noticed certain topics kept coming up time and time again (St. Leger 2020).

Tina had a remit of globalizing the HR function when coming into the role. She went on to collect lots of data and kept asking a wide range of stakeholders about what they thought HR's priorities should be involving two regional HR directors to get buy-in. Her approach was one of "honoring the past and what's been, understanding the present, and then trying to determine priorities going forward."

As you do some of the above, don't forget to reach out to your predecessor and—if appropriate—current role incumbent. Make sure you speak to them openly and establish an understanding of what they make of the role. That being said, make sure you take their input with a "pinch of salt." Depending on the circumstances and dynamics of why they are leaving or have left the role, there may be biases and viewpoints that may be only true for them.

Lastly, this is the phase where you need to think about behaviors that will help to set you up for success in your upcoming transition. It is also the time for you to reflect on how you will lead yourself, your teams, and your organization, and provides a great inflection point.

TYPICAL CHALLENGES

Typical challenges during this phase are the degree to which it's considered appropriate to get involved in organizational matters given that technically speaking you haven't started your new role yet. There may also be a challenge regarding your existing organization and the degree to which you are getting involved in your new role may be perceived as a potential issue. This is particularly the case when you are moving from one organization to another. However, I have also observed this sometimes being an issue when an executive is moving from one organization unit to another within the same company.

TYPICAL DERAILERS

A typical executive derailer at this phase is questioning whether all of the above pre-work is actually necessary. After all, as an established executive, you have been offered a top job and have been deemed the most credible candidate following what is often a rigorous assessment and selection process. Please don't fall into that trap as it may prove the biggest pitfall of your entire executive career. While past success can serve as a helpful indicator of future success, it is not necessarily the case with transitions. Make sure to leverage all of the previous, relevant experiences you have accumulated. At the same time, you also need to focus on what is required in the new role and how the organizational five Cs must be factored into your unique circumstances. As a reminder, the five Cs are:

1. Context (arguably the most important C of all, the circumstances of the organization, competition, landscape, governmental and societal)
2. Culture (organization, leadership, values)
3. Commitment (what is the organization committed to achieving for its customers, clients, and society?)
4. Circles (of influence, power, and informal decision-making)
5. Confidence (levels of employee engagement and leadership DNA)

2. IMMERSE

This is the phase often referred to as the first 90, 100, or 120 days in a new role or at the starting line (Watkins 2003; O'Keeffe 2011; Pratt 2015). Remember what I said in Chapter 2: while frameworks for the first 90, 100, or 120 days can prove to be helpful, they are simply not sufficient for the executive level.

During this phase, your key tasks are to further accelerate your understanding of the new role, the organization, its key markets, customers, suppliers, products, systems, and structures as well as people, culture, and leadership. Assuming you have done your homework during the 1.Discover phase, you can continue building on already established working relationships (or start building new ones if that is more appropriate now). Here, you will develop a deeper and more refined understanding of the situation and people. Ideally, you do this by fully immersing yourself in the surroundings of the new role.

By doing so, you will need to be very intentional to establish trust. Not only will you have to be very intentional about your potential impact early on, but you also need to start building an outstanding reputation and think about this part of the process as an investment.

You may likely come across political and cultural issues here. Be mindful of these and try to observe them for the time being and resist the urge to force an opinion or even taking a position early on. One of your key actions during this phase is to avoid organizational landmines. Think of what we learned in the previous chapter around the criticality of timing.

Also, in this phase you are shaping an initial set of priorities as well as forming first expectations and deliverables with both key stakeholders and your direct reports. Be sure to use formal sources of information as well as informal sources to educate yourself and be intentional about structuring the key elements and activities of your role. Formal sources can be your search brief or job description, your annual performance objectives, etc. Informal sources may be helpful advice from your peers, a side conversation in the boardroom with a client or with an analyst investor, etc.

You may find you have one or two gaps when it comes to being fully effective in your new executive role. Here, a key task is to work your executive network to plug any knowledge gaps to establish a better understanding of the organization, the industry, and the task at hand.

At an online panel discussion moderated by Russell Reynolds Associates in December 2020, Kathryn Pritchard, CHRO at Nord Anglia Education, was speaking about her transition experience. She recounted the most important thing for her was to:

Understand their (board) priorities because, at the end of the day, they're going to understand the business dynamics and the commercial dynamics much better than you can as a newcomer. So, whatever I thought I knew I was bringing to the role and everything I've done before, I kind of held that quite lightly, and let them lead me.

So rather than getting very sophisticated about what I thought the agenda would be, or showing them what I could do, and all of that stuff which creates anxiety, I just let them meet me really, and they gave me a very clear steer about where they wanted to go, and I let the work do the talking. That seemed to work quite well because once the work gets underway, I found I started to learn the things about the business nobody can tell you. It was all about (getting) advice points (Prichard 2020a).

Richard Demblon, Chief Human Resources Officer (CHRO) at Inchcape Shipping Services, reflected on the **2.I**mmerse phase during our interview:

As you get more senior in the roles and you move into a new role, you always have your idea of how it should be done. The hardest thing is to bide your time and really listen in that first ninety days to what is it that makes things tick, and to get some quick wins, you try and chip away as quickly as you can to establish your credibility.

That's one of the things I've learned in the more recent roles, coming into different organizations and industries. I've gone from the FMCG to mining. I've gone into rail engineering, and then I've gone to oil and gas before going into the shipping services, and each one has its strengths and weaknesses. It's not only the services and commodities that they provide, but there is also the DNA and the company mentality of what they're trying to do, with the constant being the people. There's also not one organization I've met that hasn't fallen into the trap of promoting people because they are good at what they do, rather than being good at people leadership.

To do all of the above, you'll have to plan and make time to learn, but you should also leverage your executive transition coach to support you with structured methods and tools to accelerate and de-risk your transition journey.

TYPICAL CHALLENGES

Typical challenges during this phase are the speed with which to act on apparent issues, resulting in potential risks of moving too quickly or losing credibility if an apparent indecisiveness is observed. Another challenge is the factor of time that can be wasted here.

TYPICAL DERAILERS

The typical executive derailer during this phase is to get lost in analysis paralysis. Spending too much time in the corner office studying, reading, analyzing, and mapping without being cognizant of priorities and key deliverables and you're missing out on establishing your credibility and authority when meeting with crucial stakeholders. Another derailer is not connecting and engaging with other people, or worse, connecting and being surrounded by the wrong people. Lastly, you may think you have or should have all the answers or simply try to do too many things at the same time.

3. ADAPT

This is the phase during which your inherited leadership team needs to be assessed and potentially replenished through one or more upgrades. While some research suggests you must move very quickly to establish the new leadership team within your first three months, the jury is still out as to whether pace in itself is a good measure of success (Dineen 2021c). Your executive transition coach and Human Resources leader can be great reflection partners for this. The timing of it will very much depend on your informed assessment of the inherited leadership team and when you feel the timing is right for a partial change and upgrade, bearing in mind the organizational culture, the established leadership code, and the availability of talent.

During our interview, Rudi Kindts, ex-CHRO and now executive coach, referred to the **3.A**dapt phase several months into his role and during a conversation with the Group CEO of BAT:

> *If it's true our environment is constantly changing, that means we are constantly transitioning. I'm talking about the transition we went through as a Human Resources function when it became clear we needed more organizational effectiveness (OE) capability. That's when I had to exit a long-serving HRLT member and bring in someone else as a heavyweight, with more in-depth OE experience. That was based upon the feedback that I received. It was a subtle question from Paul, the CEO, who asked me, "Rudi, do you have the team to deliver this strategy? Because your strategy is right. Budgeting is right. It's all right, but do you have the team to deliver it?" And I thought about that question. I thought, yes, but not in that (OE) area.*

There are other important actions during this phase. You have to start reconfiguring deliverables and actions based on a deeper and more refined understanding of the organization, its people, and its culture. Priorities may need to be re-assessed and as a result, some of the agreed deliverables may need to be renegotiated with key stakeholders. These could include but are not limited to people, budget, suppliers, and customer initiatives.

This phase may provide an opportunity for you to start engaging with the board. You must understand the board dynamics, priorities, areas of responsibility, and their vision for the position to which you have been appointed. The chair of the board can—in some instances—play a crucial role to also help establish this understanding.

During this phase, you also start deepening relationships with fellow executive peers. Whether it is joint site or market visits, joint conversations with key accounts, or executive leadership team off-sites, they all provide opportunities to further bond and establish a wider understanding of your peers and their roles within the organization and to learn about the business.

Make an informed decision on what you would like to be known for, what should change, and what should stay the same. As you start interacting with your line manager and fellow peers, keep a list of initiatives and practices that don't make sense to you yet. Revisit these with your line manager and executive transition coach to deepen your understanding and respectfully challenge established practices that may be unhelpful.

TYPICAL CHALLENGES

Typical challenges during this phase include appearing to be tough by replacing a few of your direct reports, or conversely, being inactive and going with the flow of the inherited leadership team and appearing to be indecisive by "playing it safe." Another challenge is a reluctance to go back and renegotiate some of the objectives or required resources to deliver against. Too many executives try to do it irrespective of the revised circumstances and new and revised data, and they lose momentum and focus as a result.

TYPICAL DERAILERS

The typical executive derailer at this phase is to fail to read, or to misread, or worse to ignore altogether the social and political cues, established cultural norms, and beliefs in the organization. Another derailer can be to stop short of changing select members of your executive leadership team, even though it may be objectively necessary and long overdue. One more derailer is to focus on the short-term, quick fixes only, and ignore aspirational and necessary long-term adjustments.

4. MOBILIZE

This is the phase that provides an opportunity for you to engage, inspire, and shine. Your first, early actions need to reconfirm to your hiring manager and the wider organization they have made the right choice by appointing the right person for the job. You must reflect on the previous phases of 1.Discover, 2.Immerse and 3.Adapt to ensure you are acting based on your reflection of learnings and understanding from the previous phases.

Here, you will need to demonstrate you have uncovered some of the underlying reasons and root causes of organizational issues and that you have identified sources of resistance to change, and selected opportunities for improved performance. You ought to emphasize that you are taking early action based on initial findings. Mobilizing the wider organization is crucial here as is building a narrative for change or transformation (whichever is necessary) to generate buy-in for what's lying ahead.

During this phase, you also need to start engaging other key stakeholders to take ownership of the diagnosis (Myszkowski 2014). Engaging talented teams of other executives to look at the same information, discuss its meaning, and arrive at similar conclusions can be an immensely powerful approach to gaining momentum and ensuring collective ownership. The additional value of engaging others to pursue the diagnostics provides an opportunity for you to evaluate who can take a fresh look at the business challenge and bring problems to light in diplomatic ways that minimize resistance to change further down the line.

During a CHRO online panel conversation organized by Russell Reynolds Associates, Kathryn Pritchard, CHRO, recalled her efforts in this way:

> About eight weeks after I had joined, we got a new chairman, and he was an ex-CHRO. As an incoming CHRO, it's like, we've got another CHRO coming in as well. Which was excellent because he started talking about the talent and the leadership agenda. He's passionate about both, and he started talking about those quite early. Even better, he's got some methodology: brilliant!

> So, that was great, because the board was instantly engaged in all of that work, and we got a dialogue going very quickly, which in turn got me going with the board quite quickly too. But the CEO needs to be very involved with that as well. You've got to keep the board and CEO, informed (Pritchard 2020b).

From a change management perspective, you can start identifying the critical mass of stakeholders who are "early adopters" and predisposed to supporting the change, the likely skeptics who will need to be constructively influenced, and the "opponents" who resist the effort and hope the initiative will eventually blow over or simply fade away. Assuming the change is successful, they will eventually either remove themselves or be removed.

TYPICAL CHALLENGES

A typical challenge during this phase is how to mobilize the parts of the organization that don't report to you, some of whom may even have different priorities and objectives. An additional challenge is finding the right balance between negotiating competing priorities with other functions (Marketing and Technology being a classic example). If you give in too much, you will be perceived as a weak negotiator and ineffective change agent. If you are forceful about your own opinion and objectives, the level of buy-in will go down and informal resistance will surge accordingly.

TYPICAL DERAILERS

A typical derailer during this phase is accepting the status quo when change is much needed. Another typical derailer at this phase is to enforce the line of command and ignore organizational realities and politics. An additional derailer is to read through job titles and positions of power when making decisions, without establishing an appreciation of the informal leaders whose opinions are considered crucial to key decision makers. Once identified, the failure may be down to not checking in with this group of critical stakeholders to get their understanding and potential opinion regarding the planned change.

5. OPERATE

This is the phase where the rubber meets the road as strategy translates into action. As a result, you and your team will need to take full, decisive, and visible action. It is likely you will face unanticipated challenges, despite having done a good job in all the above four phases. Welcome to corporate life, where things are anything but stable, with an ever-changing landscape of customers, competitors, governments, and societal needs.

You need to bear in mind error rates in change programs are much higher when team members have not worked together before. As a result, activities that help to build trust among team members and establish ways of working can serve as great investments. They can happen during the **4.Mobilize** and **5.Operate** phases. If you have attrition in the executive leadership team, such activities need to be repeated as and when you have a critical new mass in the team.

Here, cadence can serve as an integral way of working. It involves a rhythm for updates of progress and commitments, as well as deliverables to maximize performance. Here you must ensure your team is crystal clear on deliverables and that there is an established way to clarify what input, support, and outputs are required when the team meets. There must also be agreement about which decisions are to be made at the team level, and which ones require your attention and involvement.

At an online panel discussion moderated by Russell Reynolds Associates in March 2021, Sean Dineen, managing director of Russell Reynolds Associates, spoke about the executive scorecard that should have been built at the **2.I**mmerse, **3.A**dapt and **4.M**obilize phases and reviewed at this phase:

> *We know oftentimes a scorecard is a part of an assessment that's done for the CEO before they come into a portfolio company, and the ideal structured program for a CEO should last about a year and a minimum of six months. So, when we're building out that scorecard, we're usually waiting about four to six weeks until that CEO is on board.*

> *Then we're going out and we're talking to members of the deal team sponsors, the board, members of the management team, and other key stakeholders who they're going to be interfacing with and who are core to their success. We're asking them: How are they experiencing them so far? What are their expectations of them three, six, nine, and twelve months into the role?*

> *We get tangible and you get different answers from different stakeholders here, which is hugely helpful for a CEO to start to triangulate. Were things out of alignment? Does the CEO need to bring people together to have them on the same page? Where does the CEO need to start putting their focus, energies, and efforts? If we*

fast forward it a year out from now, what do you think could derail their success?

It's rare to find a CEO that's transitioning into a private equity portfolio company where they don't need to effect some sort of change. There's always going to be a change agenda, and that often requires a reshaping of the culture. So, they need to understand what does the culture look like? They also need to start to think about how that's going to shift, given our value creation plan, given our go-forward strategy. What are the mindsets, beliefs, and behaviors that need to pervade the organization to enable all of that? Where are we seeing alignment with the kind of aspirational culture we need? Where are we seeing friction? How do we get ahead of all that is invaluable.

Oftentimes, that's intelligence and data CEOs don't get as part of their transition. So having this level of intelligence, and a really quick feedback loop for a CEO, is critical, but oftentimes missing as part of the transition (Dineen 2021b).

While the **5.Mobilize** phase is likely to be full of varied activities, it also provides an opportunity for reflection. Some of the questions you can explore with your executive transition coach are:

- How do I see my function/business unit supporting the organization's strategy?

- What learnings about the successes I've had in the past can I build on? Which past failures do I need to appreciate and avoid going forward?
- Which parts of the deliverables do I need to lead? Which parts do I need to delegate to my team?
- What is the compelling message for change? What opportunities and challenges do I see emerging? What do these require of me as a leader of this organization?
- What feedback am I receiving from my line manager, peers, and other critical stakeholders on the change program? What ongoing support will I require to succeed?
- Are key stakeholders universally aligned on key priorities and performance outcomes?

TYPICAL CHALLENGES

Typical challenges during this phase are failing to sustain momentum, failing to repeat the narrative that has been established, and failing to report on quick wins and early successes. These are crucial to prove to the organization that your plan—whether changed/adapted from the initial outset or not—is actually working and, broadly speaking, on track.

TYPICAL DERAILERS

The typical executive derailer at this phase is failing to establish the right organizational structure. These can be program management office (PMO)-type resources or tribes and teams that may need to be organized in an agile way vs. the traditional hierarchical organization and job model. Another derailer can be a lack of funding and budgets, sometimes as a result of a changing business priority or issue that may be unrelated to what you're trying to establish. Another is to allow unrealistic expectations and failing to deliver on the agreed objectives.

6. NOURISH

During this phase, follow-through on reshaping actions is required as is dealing with unanticipated problems of the previous **5.Operate** phase and nipping those issues in the bud. Here you need to demonstrate that next to the quick wins already realized, some aspirational goals are close to be delivered. Ideally, you have made sure in the earlier phase they are aligned with the purpose and values of your organization.

This is also your moment to demonstrate to the organization the partial refresh and upgrade of individual leadership team members was necessary *and* the right thing to do. It will further demonstrate your orientation toward action as an executive who has an eye for exceptional talent and who is able to use judgment wisely.

It is quite likely your assessment of the previous phases, the feedback from trusted relationships, and the case for needed change will far outweigh your, and your team's capacity to deliver against. Don't fall into the trap of trying to do it all! The way you organize the work and focus on urgent key priorities will further demonstrate to the board you are the executive leader the business needs now and in the future.

Here, you need to demonstrate you have established scalable work practices to achieve balance and efficiency, and to stay present while working through adversity. Another critical element is to demonstrate and emphasize the team aspect of achieving results versus the individual heroism that takes place in some organizations.

At a CHRO online panel discussion moderated by Russell Reynolds Associates in December 2020, Ernest Marshall, executive VP HR at Eaton Corporation, spoke about his transition experience and how he made sure success was measured and acknowledged:

> *I start with that baseline, and I keep track of it, and you go about the business of doing the work. What I always do is to wait for a minimum of six months to gather feedback. That gives me two board meetings. I also ask the CEO to talk to the board members who are particularly on the committees I'm a part of, so the Compensation Committee and the Governance Committee, and say, what do they see? What do they think? So, I get their initial priorities shared with me as well.*
>
> *I have key stakeholders sitting down and doing interviews with my executive leadership team peers as well as with the HR leadership team, and then I ask the CEO to go back to the board and revisit the questions we discussed when I started. I find this process exhilarating because you understand the rhythm of the organization. It's gratifying to know you're making an impact. When I got those results back after six months, it wasn't all good. There were some things people say were stylistic, some of it was a misperception, etc. So, I do go back and talk to those people, with their permission, to clarify (Marshall 2020).*

TYPICAL CHALLENGES

Typical challenges during this phase relate to getting the balance right between learning, planning, and delivering actions.

TYPICAL DERAILERS

A typical executive derailer at this phase is to try to do more than what is objectively achievable.

7. DEVELOP

This phase of the framework focuses on a set of efforts—however small or big—to continuously improve your executive transition process. It is about you progressively learning about each phase of the process and looking for ways to improve and optimize for the next transition ahead.

Here, you will internalize your learnings and, most importantly, learn from the mistakes made along the way. This isn't just about you, though. It is also about learning through others. These may be specialists such as a business or strategy consultant, a mentor, your executive transition coach, and so forth. This could also include members of your professional network who have amassed critical experiences and thrived in similar situations and gained valuable experiences as a result.

During a Russell Reynolds webinar, Sean Dineen spoke about the learning aspects:

> *Most private equity firms are searching for that CEO who's done it before, in a private equity context. There*

is an element of safety in that approach, but the risk is you then get a CEO that's going to come in and just run the playbook: I've done this before, I'm going to do it the same way.

Any CEO transition is going to require some shifts, not only in terms of how they're thinking about the business, but also how they're relating to others. So make sure if you do a CEO assessment, the CEO gets the report. Too often, these assessments are a check the box exercise that goes into a drawer, never to be seen again.

But there are hugely valuable insights there for a CEO to learn from and think about: Where do I have some strengths and gaps? How do I need to start thinking about shifting that in this new context? Using that report to start to accelerate that is absolutely critical (Dineen 2021a).

During this phase, it is quite likely you are pushed right to the edges of your comfort zone, and in some instances, clearly outside of it. You will need to do a fair amount of reflection work as well as embodying some of the learnings going forward. Some reflective questions at this phase for you are:

- What did I achieve, and what difference did I make to the organization?
- What value did I individually, and as a team collectively, add to the business?
- Did I apply a learner/growth mindset during my transition and inspire others to do the same?

- What mistakes or misjudgments did I make along the way?
- Did I persist in the face of setbacks and seek help from others? If not, what stopped me from doing it?
- How did I prepare, support, and motivate people along the way? How did we win as a team?
- What did I learn about my strengths and development areas as well as those of my team?
- What feedback did I receive from others? What can I do with it to refine my development focus?
- Did I take the opportunity to share my learnings with anyone else? How can I make my learnings more accessible? (e.g., in form of a blog, LinkedIn post, podcast, mentorship, etc.)

At an online panel discussion moderated by Russell Reynolds Associates in December 2020, Erik Schmidt, Chief HR Officer (CHRO) at Pandora, reflected about what it took for him to be successful in CHRO roles and how crucial it is to draw upon previous experiences *and* be open-minded at the same time:

Building up to the role of CHRO, during the preparation, there are probably two big things that stand out for me. One is to make sure you've built the breadth in your experience, as you're going to need it.

When I look back on my twenty-five years and in a variety of different companies, there isn't an element from all of them I haven't used in the CHRO roles. People expect you to know things on the spot, so you need to have that at your fingertips.

Secondly, when you don't have it at your fingertips, you should have a very well-developed network of people around you, trusted advisers, specialists, colleagues, and peers you can tap into and say: Hey, can somebody help me out with this particular topic? (Schmidt 2020).

TYPICAL CHALLENGES

A typical challenge during this phase is to cut down on, or skip, this phase entirely. After all, there is so much to do, and you may think post-mortems and reflections are for NASA scientists. It is hard, and as a modern executive, you will continuously be pressed for time. While useful at a conceptual level (it will be hard to disagree with this, quite frankly), if you took the time to do the above reflections to embody some of the key learnings, you may not have the time to reflect on other aspects, important actions, and initiatives, and clearly you are an executive who is in high demand.

TYPICAL DERAILERS

A typical executive derailer at this phase is to get carried away by daily activities and fighting fires instead of "sharpening the saw."

This is by far the longest chapter of this book. We looked at the Double Diamond Framework© of Executive Transitions, its seven phases, as well as typical challenges and derailers during each phase. Depending on the unique circumstance of the executive, they may also be jumping between converging and diverging, and at times, even jumping one or two phases altogether.

In the next chapter, we'll look at how to successfully transition out of an executive role.

CHAPTER 14

HOW TO SUCCESSFULLY TRANSITION OUT OF AN EXECUTIVE ROLE

———

As we have already discovered in this book, while focusing on the first 90–120 days is crucial for any executive starting a new role, it isn't sufficient. It is often overlooked that the last 90–120 days in an executive role are equally important. The same applies to popular literature and general research done in this space. When googling "Making the most of your first 90 days" the search engine delivered over 9.3 billion results in October 2020. Whereas "Making the most of your last 90 days" delivered only 57 million results, less than 1 percent of that.

As an outgoing executive, you ought to continue to act in a manner that would enhance the chances of leaving behind a leadership legacy that outlasts your tenure in the organization. What most executives don't realize is their legacy is often fully defined only *after* they have departed from the organization.

Many executives worry that as soon as their departure has been announced, they become "lame duck" executives. Anton Fishman, one of the interviewees in my book, referred to this phenomenon during our conversation:

"With some executives, during their last ninety days other members of the organization have already started to ignore them or stopped talking about them, or stopped inviting them to critical meetings."

However, as the former Ecolab CEO Doug Baker, who had been in the role for sixteen years, puts it, the advice is to "run through the finishing line." He would know. He is considered one of the best-performing CEOs globally (George 2019). He ranked in the top forty of *CEO 100*, *HBR*'s annual study on best-performing CEOs (Citrin, Hildebrand, and Stark 2019).

Often, you will be aware of when you will be leaving your current role, and sometimes that means leaving the organization. At the senior level, notice periods of six to twelve months aren't unusual. Sometimes this leads the incumbent to go into a "freeze mode," with a natural tendency to step back from making any major decisions. If that is genuinely the best objective action in your unique circumstances, then that's fine, but what if it isn't? The same may apply in the case where an internal successor has been identified and is meant to take over from you in the foreseeable future. Naturally, stepping on the toes of your successor is something you would ideally like to avoid, but it may be necessary or even required.

My advice is you need to assess whether there are any major initiatives or decisions that *must be taken before you depart.* This needs to be done in a way that is consistent with your authentic leadership style and in line with the organization's culture and established norms and beliefs.

The subject of "Your Last 90 Days" hasn't been researched well enough to provide meaningful guidance; however, a McKinsey article focusses on some key questions outgoing executives can ask themselves before departing (Caspar and Halbye 2011). I have further enriched these with my own experience working with executive transition coaching clients. I have also answered these in a way to show how they can help the incoming executive as well as the outgoing one.

WOULD I UNDERTAKE ANY MAJOR DECISIONS IF I HAD ANOTHER THREE YEARS AHEAD OF ME?

As the incumbent, you are naturally insightful about the strengths and weaknesses of your organization's current strategy and operations, and your own function. If you, as the outgoing executive, stop acting and if we assume it will take the incoming executive a few months to understand their role, the organizational set up, culture, etc., then an entire year could pass before any major decision is taken. This one-year delay could prove costly in many industries, and in others, result in a loss of market share down the line.

WHICH PEOPLE-RELATED DECISIONS WOULD I MAKE IF I COULD STAY FOR THREE MORE YEARS?

As an executive, you naturally care about the bench strength of your organization's talent and pay particular attention to the makeup of your executive leadership team. Frequent upgrades with the support of the Human Resources function are very common. Imagine if you left the tough and often unpopular people decisions to your successor. An excuse I have sometimes come across is the incoming executive should be making their people assessment and are free to build their own ideal executive leadership team.

However, there is a unique disadvantage built into this thinking. First, the incoming executive is always free to make changes to their executive leadership team anyhow. Second, they would benefit immensely from having a high-performing leadership team right from the outset. So, if a tough people decision needs to be taken, then take it—as it will give the incoming executive both a clean slate and the best chance of succeeding.

At an online panel discussion moderated by Russell Reynolds Associates in March 2021, Sean Dineen, managing director of Russell Reynolds Associates, spoke of the importance of the executive leadership team:

> One of the biggest mistakes is for an organization to say we'll wait until the CEO gets on board, and they can deal with some of the issues on the (executive leadership) team. If you know you have an issue on the team—say, somebody is underperforming—take care of it before the CEO comes on board. Don't leave

*them a fantasy that they need to go and fix which you
already know is there. So start to address that proac-
tively (Dineen 2021).*

DO WE HAVE ADEQUATE OPERATIONAL EXCELLENCE AND MOMENTUM TO DELIVER STRONG RESULTS THIS YEAR AND NEXT YEAR?

Given the constantly changing landscape, organizations
need to both create and respond to the changing business
dynamics to effectively serve their customers. As an outgoing
executive, you must ensure your function and organization
have a rigorously aligned set of activities to drive and shape
ongoing change while building new capabilities that are
required now and in the future.

As an example, companies have often externally communi-
cated cost-saving initiatives that run over multiple years. If
targets are met and achieved earlier than planned, this will
leave the incoming executive with a more manageable cost
base to work with and avoid being on the backpedal with
external investors and major shareholders.

Another issue is the "momentum freeze" that kicks in when
a new executive is being onboarded. Often the senior leaders
will want to observe and understand what the new C-level
leader is like, and which preferences they have, before making suggestions to change existing processes or launch major
initiatives. I have observed this myself when all coaching
initiatives in an organization were put on hold, only to see
whether the incoming Chief HR Officer values coaching as
a developmental instrument or not. Not only did we lose

crucial momentum that had been carefully built up before that point, but the topic was also put off by over two years as other priorities emerged that required funding.

The period of momentum freeze leads, at least in part, to lost productivity and, in a worst-case scenario, even lost market share. It can be avoided by having a detailed plan shared between you as the outgoing executive and your successor with clear accountabilities, performance milestones, who owns what, and who is the executive sponsor of which initiative. At the C-level, this plan should also be transparently shared with the management or supervisory board, so all directors have a common knowledge of where the company stands and are able to act as accountability partners to both executives.

WHAT IS MY GREATEST SINGLE CONCERN AND HOW WOULD I GO ABOUT SOLVING IT, IF I HAD ANOTHER THREE YEARS LEFT?

This speaks to the power of one. Whether it is a lack of talent bench, slow digitalization effort, lack of revenue growth, an activist investor, etc., the list of things that could keep you up at night can be long. While as an outgoing executive you will have many battlegrounds and issues to attend to, there usually is one "thing" that keeps you up at night most of all.

Given the constantly changing landscape, organizations need to both create momentum and respond to the changing business dynamics to effectively serve their customers. As an outgoing executive, you are best served to share the issue with your successor and may even have a few high-level ideas on what to do about it, if you had had more time to do so.

WITH THE BENEFIT OF HINDSIGHT, WHAT ADVICE WOULD I HAVE GIVEN TO MYSELF WHEN STARTING IN THIS ROLE?

Despite the size and scale of global organizations, organizational knowledge is often kept in mysterious ways with a few key incumbents. These may or may not be obvious stakeholders to an incoming executive. As a result, you, as the outgoing executive, have a crucial role to play by sharing the list of names deemed to be crucial conversation partners with the incoming executive.

This list often includes people who may not be obvious candidates for a conversation with the incoming executive. They could include external stakeholders, such as the largest customers (key accounts), a select number of shareholders, or governmental officials. They could also be other stakeholders who may not be obvious to your successor, such as a retired chairman, investors, one or two members of the founding family of the company that usually don't get involved in the daily running of the business, etc.

The same applies to the established organizational culture. Sometimes what is printed on posters in the head office as "our cultural values" isn't necessarily an accurate reflection of the true culture of an organization. Again, you and the other key stakeholders have a crucial role to play to help the incoming executive avoid cultural landmines making sure they don't create a wrong first impression, particularly with the wider organization.

The Chief HR Officer of one of the largest and most successful software companies in the world had to step down in less than a year of being appointed to the executive management team after the press had leaked details about her weekly commute between the corporate head office and her hometown using the corporate jet (Dammann 2011). While this was a contractually granted benefit, it was deemed highly inappropriate as that same organization had taken a sustainability pledge, both internally and externally. The granted benefit wasn't much aligned with the established culture of the firm. Once this issue had been made public, the pressure grew quickly and the C-level leader left the company.

WHY WOULD I CARE ABOUT MY LAST 90–120 DAYS?

It may be obvious delivering a great set of actions during your last 90–120 days requires focused determination and might even appear to be partially stepping on the toes of your successor, and something you would prefer to avoid.

That being said, research and my own experience of working with senior executives on their last 90–120 days demonstrate it can pay huge dividends, not least to your legacy as an executive leader. It will serve as a precious gift both to the organization and to your successor. Furthermore, your reputation will most likely be noted in future job situations and positively impact the future trajectory of your executive career.

Just remind yourself of the sleepless nights you had when you took over from a predecessor who didn't much care during their last months or weeks in the role. How much better would it have been for you as the incoming executive *and* for the outgoing executive if both of you were satisfied you did all you possibly could until the very last day in the executive office?

If you think now is a little early to start planning for your departure, be reminded of the best practice recommended by Russell Reynolds Associates. In a 2013 article, Rusty O'Kelley, who is the global leader of their board advisory and effectiveness practice, recommends CEO successions should be a long-term project (three to four years) and take about 10 percent of the time of the newly appointed CEO.

Erik Schmidt, Chief HR Officer at Pandora, described his experience of onboarding in our interview as follows:

> *What do I need to get done in the first thirty days to build credibility? Where are the fires? Frankly, you know if your predecessor was asked to leave, then you know what's happened. There are going to be fires, either things the predecessor hasn't finished, or there are things they didn't want to talk about or raise."*

HOW DO I TREAT MY SUCCESSOR (OR PREDECESSOR) WITH DUE RESPECT AND ENSURE BUY-IN?

At an online panel discussion moderated by Russell Reynolds Associates in December 2020, Trui Hebbelinck, CHRO at LivaNova, described her experience when taking over from her predecessor who had been in a chief administrative officer (CAO) role in corporate Human Resources for about fifteen years:

> *My predecessor had been with the company more than fifteen years, as a CAO—a general counsel with a bit of HR and IT on the side. Part of the attraction of the job for me was to be able to establish HR right from the start. But there was another established HR Director who was pretty much used to doing things in a certain way. So, if you're ever in that situation, it's a luxury to have a predecessor—that is, one who's looking forward to having somebody to take over from them but at the same time, is happy to let go.*
>
> *Speaking with the CEO, he wanted to see a very clear talent strategy going forward and an HR strategy for the future of the company, which wasn't there. So, I knew those strategies needed to be built, but where do you start? So I asked the previous CAO a lot of questions before I started, and there was psychology at play as well. While he was very receptive to the handover— he was retiring—he still had to step back and allow somebody else to take over, which is not always easy. So treading all my questions very carefully with respect for him, and for the team around him, paid dividends (Hebbelinck 2020).*

WHAT SHOULD BE MY PLAN FOR MY LAST 90–120 DAYS?

I hope the above reflective questions provide you with an opportunity to spend some time making a robust plan for your last 90–120 days. You can also use the Double Diamond Framework© of Executive Transitions for this. All you have to do is to skip the **1.Discover**, **2.Immerse**, and **3.Adapt** phases and begin with **4.Mobilize**, **5.Operate**, and **6.Nourish** before moving to **7.Develop**.

THE DOUBLE DIAMOND FRAMEWORK© OF EXECUTIVE TRANSITIONS

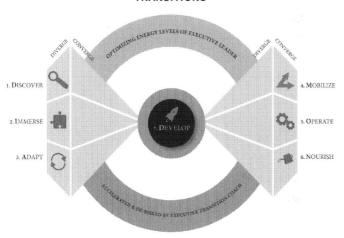

Figure 14.1. The Double Diamond Framework© of Executive Transitions by Navid Nazemian Executive Coaching (Nazemian 2021).

THE END: A BRIEF RECAP OF THIS BOOK

In the first part of this book—**Foundations**—we looked at the history of executive transitions, followed by the science and intentionality of onboarding frameworks. We then took a look at why this is a topical subject right now before looking at key differences between transition advisers and leadership development coaches.

In the second part of the book—**Challenges & Failures**—we looked at existing organizational onboarding frameworks, followed by the top ten reasons for executive transition failure. Then I highlighted the true cost of failed executive transitions before exploring key executive transition challenges rooted in people, culture, business, or technical issues.

In the third part of the book—**Toward Transition Mastery**—we talked about the compelling business case for getting executive transitions right. This was followed with key interventions to make executive transitions more successful. I then introduced you to the Double Diamond Framework© of Executive Transitions before walking you through the seven phases and highlighted typical challenges and derailers at each phase.

The fourth and last part of the book—**Your Last 90 Days**—looks at how to successfully transition out of an executive role.

It has taken me seven years from start to finish in writing this book to follow my passion of supporting executives during critical transitions, and I am always inspired by their courage to deliver value to their organization while staying true to their authentic selves.

—NAVID NAZEMIAN

Do get in touch with me if you have any comments, feedback or questions: hello@masteringexecutivetransitions.com

APPENDIX

———

INTRODUCTION

Bradt, George, and Gillian Davis. *First-Time Leader: Foundational Tools for Inspiring and Enabling Your New Team.* Hoboken: Wiley, 2014.

Bradt, George, Jayme A. Check, and Jorge E. Pedraza. *The New Leader's 100-Day Action Plan: How to Take Charge, Build or Merge Your Team, and Get Immediate Results.* New York, John Wiley & Sons, Inc., 2011.

Burroughs, Michael K. *Before Onboarding: How to Integrate New Leaders for Quick and Sustained Results.* Createspace Independent Publishing Platform, 2011.

Byford, Mark, Michael D. Watkins, and Lena Triantogiannis. "Onboarding Isn't Enough." *Harvard Business Review*, May–June 2017. https://hbr.org/2017/05/onboarding-isnt-enough.

Ciampa, Dan, and Michael D. Watkins. *Right from the Start: Taking Charge in a New Leadership Role.* Massachusetts: Harvard Business Publishing, 1999.

Ciampa, Dan, and David Dotlich. *Transitions at the Top: What Organizations Must Do to Make Sure New Leaders Succeed.* San Francisco: Jossey-Bass, 2015.

Dineen, Sean. "De-Risking Executive Transitions to Accelerate Value Creation." March 9, 2021. Russell Reynolds and Hunt Scanlon Media. Virtual Webinar, 11:09. https://huntscanlon. com/webinars/de-risking-executive-transitions-to-accelerate-value-creation/.

Exechange. *Exechange News*. Frankfurt: Daniel Schauber Media: 2020.

Goldsmith, Marshall. *What Got You Here Won't Get You There*. London: Profile Books, 2008.

International Institute for Management Development. "Michael Watkins: Leadership Transitions." IMD Faculty. Accessed September 2, 2021. https://www.imd.org/faculty/professors/michael-watkins.

Keller, Scott and Mary Meaney. "Successfully Transitioning to New Leadership Roles." *McKinsey & Company*, May 23, 2018. https://www.veruspartners.net/wp-content/uploads/2018/06/Successfully-transitioning-to-new-leadership-roles-web-final.pdf.

O'Keeffe, Niamh. *Your First 100 Days: Make Maximum Impact in Your New Role*. New Jersey: Pearson Education, 2011.

Watkins, Michael D. *Master Your Next Move: The Essential Companion to "The First 90 Days."* Massachusetts: Harvard Business Publishing, 2019.

Watkins, Michael D. *The First 90 Days: Critical Success Strategies for New Leaders at All Levels*. Massachusetts: Harvard Business Publishing, 2003.

Watkins, Michael D. *Your Next Move: The Leader's Guide to Navigating Major Career Transitions*. Massachusetts: Harvard Business Publishing, 2009.

CHAPTER 1—HISTORY OF EXECUTIVE TRANSITIONS

Chandran, Rajiv, and Hortense de la Boutetiere, and Carolyn Dewar. "Ascending to the C-suite." *McKinsey & Company*,

April 1, 2015. https://www.mckinsey.com/featured-insights/ leadership/ascending-to-the-c-suite.

Fatemi, Falon. "The True Cost of a Bad Hire—It's More Than You Think." *Forbes,* Sep 28, 2016. https://www.forbes.com/sites/ falonfatemi/2016/09/28/the-true-cost-of-a-bad-hire-its-more- than-you-think/?sh=12f6dbe4aa41.

Keller, Scott and Mary Meaney. "Successfully Transitioning to New Leadership Roles." *McKinsey & Company,* May 23, 2018. https:// www.veruspartners.net/wp-content/uploads/2018/06/Success- fully-transitioning-to-new-leadership-roles-web-final.pdf.

Masters, Brooke. "Rise of a Headhunter." *Financial Times,* March 30, 2009. https://www.ft.com/content/19975256-1af2-11de-8aa3- 0000779fd2ac.

Watkins, Michael D. *The First 90 Days: Critical Success Strategies for New Leaders at All Levels.* Massachusetts: Harvard Business Publishing, 2003.

CHAPTER 2—THE SCIENCE OF INTENTIONALITY & FRAMEWORKS

Birshan, Michael, Thomas Meakin, and Kurt Strovink. "How New CEOs Can Boost Their Odds of Success." *McKinsey & Company,* May 20, 2016. https://www.mckinsey.com/fea- tured-insights/leadership/how-new-ceos-can-boost-their- odds-of-success.

Bradt, George. "The Top Five Executive Onboarding and Leader- ship Ideas from My First 700 Forbes Articles." *PrimeGenesis* (blog). Accessed May 5, 2021. https://www.primegenesis.com/ our-blog/2021/04/the-top-five-executive-onboarding-and- leadership-ideas-from-my-first-700-forbes-articles/.

Burroughs, Michael K. *Before Onboarding: How to Integrate New Leaders for Quick and Sustained Results*. Createspace Independent Publishing Platform, 2011.

Byford, Mark, Michael D. Watkins, and Lena Triantogiannis. "Onboarding Isn't Enough." *Harvard Business Review*, May–June 2017. https://hbr.org/2017/05/onboarding-isnt-enough.

Byrne, John A. "The Fast Company Interview: Jeff Immelt." *Fast Company*, July, 1, 2005. https://www.fastcompany.com/53574/fast-company-interview-jeff-immelt.

Caspar, Christian, and Michael Halbye. "Making the Most of the CEO's Last 100 Days." *McKinsey & Company*, January 1, 2011. https://www.mckinsey.com/featured-insights/leadership/making-the-most-of-the-ceos-last-100-days.

Chandran, Rajiv, and Hortense de la Boutetiere, and Carolyn Dewar. "Ascending to the C-suite." *McKinsey & Company*, April 1, 2015. https://www.mckinsey.com/featured-insights/leadership/ascending-to-the-c-suite.

Keller, Scott and Mary Meaney. "Successfully Transitioning to New Leadership Roles." *McKinsey & Company*, May 23, 2018. https://www.veruspartners.net/wp-content/uploads/2018/06/Successfully-transitioning-to-new-leadership-roles-web-final.pdf.

Muoio, Danielle. "Former GE CEO Jeff Immelt Used to Have an Empty Private Jet Fly Next to His—Just in Case There Were Delays." *Business Insider: India:* October, 18, 2017. https://www.businessinsider.in/former-ge-ceo-jeff-immelt-used-to-have-an-empty-private-jet-fly-next-to-his---just-in-case-there-were-delays/articleshow/61138682.cms.

Shen, Lucinda. "General Electric's Value Plummeted Under CEO Jeff Immelt." *Fortune,* June 12, 2017. https://fortune.com/2017/06/12/ge-stock-jeff-immelt/.

Triantogiannis, Lena. "Egon Zehnder and The First 90 Days Author Release Onboarding Effectiveness Assessment to Improve New

Executive Integration." *EgonZehnder,* April 18, 2017. https://
www.egonzehnder.com/press-release/egon-zehnder-and-the-
first-90-days-author-release-onboarding-effectiveness-assess-
ment-to-improve-new-executive-integration.

Watkins, Michael D. "An Interview with Harvard Business Review
Press Executive Editor." Accessed on October 15, 2021. Genesis. Virtual Webinar, 10:30. https://news.genesisadvisers.com/
harvard-business-review-press-executive-editor-jeff-kehoe-in-
terviews-michael-watkins-about-career-transitions.

Watkins, Michael D. "Does Your Company Really Do a Good Job
of Onboarding New Hires?" International Institute for Management Development (IMD), June 2017a. https://www.imd.
org/research-knowledge/articles/does-your-company-really-
do-a-good-job-of-onboarding-new-hires/.

Watkins, Michael D. *How Transition Coaches Accelerate Executive
Onboarding.* Lausanne: International Institute for Management
Development, 2017b.

Watkins, Michael D. *Master Your Next Move: The Essential Companion to "The First 90 Days."* Massachusetts: Harvard Business
Publishing, 2019.

Wheeler, Patricia. *Executive Transitions Market Study Summary
Report: 2008.* The Institute of Executive Development and
Alexcel Group, 2008. https://www.slideshare.net/harv6pack/
executivetransitionsmarketstudyreportpw.

Wheeler, Patricia. "Senior Leadership Transitions: What Makes
Them Work and What Causes Them to Fail?" *Business Coaching
Worldwide,* October 2009. https://wabccoaches.com/2009/09/
senior-leadership-transitions-what-makes-them-work-and-
what-causes-them-to-fail/.

CHAPTER 3—WHY NOW?

Anders, George, Fereshteh Amini, Assembly, Callie August, Nancy Baym, Darcy Cain, Anbu Chinnasamy, Mary Donohue, Murat Erer, Godfrey Dadich Partners, Amber Hoak, Sonia Jaffe, Karin Kimbrough, Jonathan Larson, Laura Lorenzetti Soper, Ronnie Martin, Hannah McConnaughey, Gale Moutrey, Plain Concepts, Loren Pokorny, Sharat Raghavan, Sean Rintel, Colette Stallbaumer, Kim Stocks, David Titsworth, WE Communications, and Jessica Voelker. *2021 Work Trend Index: Annual Report: The Next Great Disruption Is Hybrid Work—Are We Ready?* Redmond: Microsoft Corporation, 2021. https://www.microsoft.com/en-us/worklab/work-trend-index/hybrid-work.

Association of Executive Search and Leadership Consultants. *BlueSteps 2013 Executive Mobility Report—May 2013.* New York: BlueSteps, 2013. https://www.aesc.org/insights/thought-leadership/aesc-insights/bluesteps-2013-executive-mobility-report-may-2013.

Baldoni, John. "How To Help New Executives Succeed." *Harvard Business Review,* May 05, 2008. https://hbr.org/2008/05/how-to-help-new-executives-suc.

Bersin, Josh. "Not Enough Workers: Rethink Recruiting in the New Economy." *Josh Bersin* (blog), May 2, 2021. https://joshbersin.com/2021/05/not-enough-workers-rethink-recruiting-in-the-new-economy/.

Bureau of Labor Statistics. "The Employment Situation—September 2021." US Department of Labor press release, October 8, 2021. Bureau of Labor Statistics website. https://www.bls.gov/news.release/pdf/empsit.pdf.

Chappell, Joe. "More than One-Third of Senior Executives Worldwide Expect to Transition Industries in the Next Three Years." *Business Wire,* June 4, 2013. https://www.businesswire.com/

news/home/20130604006425/en/More-than-One-Third-of-Senior-Executives-Worldwide-Expect-to-Transition-Industries-in-the-Next-Three-Years.

Ciampa, Dan, and David Dotlich. *Transitions at the Top: What Organizations Must Do to Make Sure New Leaders Succeed.* San Francisco: Jossey-Bass, 2015.

Development Dimensions International. *Leadership Transitions Report 2021.* Bridgeville: Development Dimensions International, May 19, 2021. https://www.ddiworld.com/research/leadership-transitions-report.

Dineen, Sean. "De-Risking Executive Transitions to Accelerate Value Creation." March 9, 2021. Russell Reynolds and Hunt Scanlon Media. Virtual Webinar, 11:02. https://huntscanlon.com/webinars/de-risking-executive-transitions-to-accelerate-value-creation/.

Fortune. "Fortune 500." Rankings. Accessed October 14, 2021.

Kane, Phillip and Grace Ocean. "The Great Resignation Is Here, and It's Real." *Inc.,* August 26, 2021. https://www.inc.com/phillip-kane/the-great-resignation-is-here-its-real.html.

Keller, Scott and Mary Meaney. "Successfully Transitioning to New Leadership Roles." *McKinsey & Company,* May 23, 2018. https://www.veruspartners.net/wp-content/uploads/2018/06/Successfully-transitioning-to-new-leadership-roles-web-final.pdf.

Leading Effectively Staff. "Developing Talent? You're Probably Missing Vertical Development." *The Center for Creative Leadership* (blog), November 25, 2020. https://www.ccl.org/articles/leading-effectively-articles/developing-talent-youre-probably-missing-vertical-development/.

Morieux, Yves. "Smart Rules: Six Ways to Get People to Solve Problems Without You." *Harvard Business Review,* September 2011. https://hbr.org/2011/09/smart-rules-six-ways-to-get-people-to-solve-problems-without-you.

Nawaz, Sabina. "The Biggest Mistakes New Executives Make." *Harvard Business Review*, May 15, 2017. https://hbr.org/2017/05/the-biggest-mistakes-new-executives-make.

Neilson, Gary L., and Julie Wulf. "How Many Direct Reports?" *Harvard Business Review*, April 2012. https://hbr.org/2012/04/how-many-direct-reports.

Paese, Matt. "Private Struggle: Why Executive Transitions Continue to Fail." *Development Dimensions International* (blog), May 19, 2021. https://www.ddiworld.com/blog/executive-transitions.

Thackray, Richard. "De-Risking Executive Transitions to Accelerate Value Creation." March 9, 2021. Russell Reynolds and Hunt Scanlon Media. Virtual Webinar, 8:18. https://huntscanlon.com/webinars/de-risking-executive-transitions-to-accelerate-value-creation/.

Torres, Roselinde, and Peter Tollman. *Debunking the Myths of the First 100 Days*. Boston: Boston Consulting Group, 2013. https://nanopdf.com/download/debunking-the-myths-of-the-first-100-days-the-right-way-and-the_pdf#.

Warren, Jeff. "De-Risking Executive Transitions to Accelerate Value Creation." March 9, 2021. Russell Reynolds and Hunt Scanlon Media. Virtual Webinar, 6:44-6:48. https://huntscanlon.com/webinars/de-risking-executive-transitions-to-accelerate-value-creation/.

Watkins, Michael D. *The First 90 Days: Critical Success Strategies for New Leaders at All Levels*. Massachusetts: Harvard Business Publishing, 2003.

Yu, Sun. "China Set to Report First Population Decline in Five Decades." *Financial Times*, April 27, 2021. https://www.ft.com/content/008ea78a-8bc1-4954-b283-700608d3dc6c.

CHAPTER 4—THE DIFFERENCE BETWEEN TRANSITION ADVISORS & LEADERSHIP DEVELOPMENT COACHES

Bradt, George, Jayme A. Check, and Jorge E. Pedraza. *The New Leader's 100-Day Action Plan: How to Take Charge, Build or Merge Your Team, and Get Immediate Results.* New York, John Wiley & Sons, Inc, 2011.

Burroughs, Michael K. *Before Onboarding: How to Integrate New Leaders for Quick and Sustained Results.* Createspace Independent Publishing Platform, 2011.

Covey, Stephen R. *The 7 Habits of Highly Effective People.* New York: Simon & Schuster, 2020.

International Institute for Management Development. "Executive Onboarding Effectiveness Assessment." Accessed October 14, 2021. https://assessments.genesisadvisers.com/imd.

Keller, Scott and Mary Meaney. "Successfully Transitioning to New Leadership Roles." *McKinsey & Company,* May 23, 2018. https://www.veruspartners.net/wp-content/uploads/2018/06/Successfully-transitioning-to-new-leadership-roles-web-final.pdf.

Watkins, Michael D. *How Transition Coaches Accelerate Executive Onboarding.* Lausanne: International Institute for Management Development, 2017.

Watkins, Michael D. *Master Your Next Move: The Essential Companion to "The First 90 Days."* Massachusetts: Harvard Business Publishing, 2019.

Watkins, Michael D. *The First 90 Days: Critical Success Strategies for New Leaders at All Levels.* Massachusetts: Harvard Business Publishing, 2003.

CHAPTER 5—ORGANIZATIONAL ONBOARDING FRAMEWORKS

Byford, Mark, Michael D. Watkins, and Lena Triantogiannis. "Onboarding Isn't Enough." *Harvard Business Review*, May–June 2017. https://hbr.org/2017/05/onboarding-isnt-enough.

Chandran, Rajiv, and Hortense de la Boutetiere, and Carolyn Dewar. "Ascending to the C-suite." *McKinsey & Company*, April 1, 2015. https://www.mckinsey.com/featured-insights/leadership/ascending-to-the-c-suite.

Development Dimensions International. *Leadership Transitions Report 2021*. Bridgeville: Development Dimensions International, May 19, 2021. https://www.ddiworld.com/research/leadership-transitions-report.

Dineen, Sean. "De-Risking Executive Transitions to Accelerate Value Creation." March 9, 2021. Russell Reynolds and Hunt Scanlon Media. Virtual Webinar, 11:24. https://huntscanlon.com/webinars/de-risking-executive-transitions-to-accelerate-value-creation/.

Gaines-Ross, Leslie. *CEO Capital: A Guide to Building CEO Reputation and Company Success*. Hoboken: Wiley, 2002.

Grothaus, M. "The Floppy Disk Is Dead (And Apple Helped Kill It)." *Engadeget*, April 28th, 2010.

Keller, Scott and Mary Meaney. "Successfully Transitioning to New Leadership Roles." *McKinsey & Company*, May 23, 2018. https://www.veruspartners.net/wp-content/uploads/2018/06/Successfully-transitioning-to-new-leadership-roles-web-final.pdf.

Marshall, Ernest. "De-Risking Executive Transitions to Accelerate Value Creation." March 9, 2021. Russell Reynolds and Hunt Scanlon Media. Virtual Webinar, 52:59. https://huntscanlon.com/webinars/de-risking-executive-transitions-to-accelerate-value-creation/.

Microsoft Corporation. "Office 97 FAQs from Support Online." Docs: TechNet Archive: Tips. February 20, 2014.

Murphy, Mark. "Leadership IQ Study: Why New Hires Fail." *CIS-ION: PRWeb*. Washington DC: PRWeb, 2005.

Smart, Brad, and Geoff Smart. *Topgrading (How To Hire, Coach and Keep A Players)*. Dallas: Pritchett, 2005.

Steeber, Michael. "A Decade without Discs: The Original Macbook Air Turns 10 Today." *9TO5Mac*, January 15, 2018. https://9to-5mac.com/2018/01/15/macbook-air-10-years/.

Triantogiannis, Lena, and Mark Byford. "Onboarding Isn't Enough: Executives Need To Be Fully Integrated Into Your Culture." *EgonZehnder*, April 19, 2017. https://www.egonzehnder.com/what-we-do/leadership-advisory/accelerated-integration/insights/onboarding-isnt-enough-executives-need-to-be-fully-integrated-into-your-culture.

Watkins, Michael D. "Internal Hires Need Just as Much Support as External Ones." *Harvard Business Review*, April 4, 2016. https://hbr.org/2016/04/internal-hires-need-just-as-much-support-as-external-ones.

Westfall, Chris. "Leadership Development Is a $366 Billion Industry: Here's Why Most Programs Don't Work." *Forbes*, June 20, 2019. https://www.forbes.com/sites/chriswestfall/2019/06/20/leadership-development-why-most-programs-dont-work/?sh=7c81cb061de4.

Wheeler, Patricia. *Executive Transitions Market Study Summary Report: 2008*. The Institute of Executive Development and Alexcel Group, 2008. https://www.slideshare.net/harv6pack/executivetransitionsmarketstudyreportpw.

CHAPTER 6—THE TOP 10 REASONS FOR EXECUTIVE TRANSITION FAILURE

Bradt, George. "Don't Lead Until You Have Earned the Right to Lead in a New Job." *Forbes,* May 15, 2012a. https://www.forbes.com/sites/georgebradt/2012/05/15/dont-lead-until-you-have-earned-the-right-to-lead-in-a-new-job/?sh=7eae3a51108f.

Bradt, George. "Heidrick and Struggles Study of 20,000 Searches Highlights Need for Onboarding Improvements." *Prime-Genesis* (blog). Accessed October 14, 2021b. https://www.primegenesis.com/our-blog/2009/04/40-percent-of-execs-pushed-out-fail-or-quit-within-18-months/.

Byford, Mark, Michael D. Watkins, and Lena Triantogiannis. "Onboarding Isn't Enough." *Harvard Business Review,* May–June 2017. https://hbr.org/2017/05/onboarding-isnt-enough.

Craighill, Kenly. "The Jack Welch Legacy: Rank It, or Yank It?" *Woden, March 19, 2020.* https://wodenworks.medium.com/the-jack-welch-legacy-rank-it-or-yank-it-869e0fb9ff63.

Dineen, Sean. "De-Risking Executive Transitions to Accelerate Value Creation." March 9, 2021a. Russell Reynolds and Hunt Scanlon Media. Virtual Webinar, 10:20. https://huntscanlon.com/webinars/de-risking-executive-transitions-to-accelerate-value-creation/.

Dineen, Sean. "De-Risking Executive Transitions to Accelerate Value Creation." March 9, 2021b. Russell Reynolds and Hunt Scanlon Media. Virtual Webinar, 11:20-11:53. https://huntscanlon.com/webinars/de-risking-executive-transitions-to-accelerate-value-creation/.

Dineen, Sean. "De-Risking Executive Transitions to Accelerate Value Creation." March 9, 2021c. Russell Reynolds and Hunt Scanlon Media. Virtual Webinar, 28.40. https://huntscanlon.com/webinars/de-risking-executive-transitions-to-accelerate-value-creation/.

Fisher, Anne. "New Job? Get a Head Start Now." *Fortune* (blog), February 17, 2021. https://fortune.com/2012/02/17/new-job-get-a-head-start-now/.

Gara, Antoine. "For GE's Jeff Immelt, Hundreds Of Deals And $575 Billion Didn't Yield A Higher Stock Price." *Forbes,* June 15, 2017. https://www.forbes.com/sites/antoinegara/2017/06/15/for-ges-jeff-immelt-hundreds-of-deals-and-575-billion-didnt-yield-a-higher-stock-price/?sh=15b511b97226.

Goleman, Daniel. *Emotional Intelligence: Why It Can Matter More Than IQ.* New York: Bantam, 1995.

Keller, Scott and Mary Meaney. "Successfully Transitioning to New Leadership Roles." *McKinsey & Company,* May 23, 2018. https://www.veruspartners.net/wp-content/uploads/2018/06/Successfully-transitioning-to-new-leadership-roles-web-final.pdf

Masters, Brooke. "Rise of a Headhunter." *Financial Times,* March 30, 2009. https://www.ft.com/content/19975256-1af2-11de-8aa3-0000779fd2ac.

Murphy, Mark. "Leadership IQ Study: Why New Hires Fail." *CISION: PRWeb.* Washington DC: PRWeb, 2005.

Smart, Brad, and Geoff Smart. *Topgrading (How To Hire, Coach and Keep A Players).* Dallas: Pritchett, 2005.

Triantogiannis, Lena, and Mark Byford. "Onboarding Isn't Enough: Executives Need To Be Fully Integrated Into Your Culture." *EgonZehnder,* April 19, 2017. https://www.egonzehnder.com/what-we-do/leadership-advisory/accelerated-integration/insights/onboarding-isnt-enough-executives-need-to-be-fully-integrated-into-your-culture.

Wheeler, Patricia. *Executive Transitions Market Study Summary Report: 2008.* The Institute of Executive Development and Alexcel Group, 2008. https://www.slideshare.net/harv6pack/executivetransitionsmarketstudyreportpw.

CHAPTER 7—THE TRUE COST OF FAILED EXECUTIVE TRANSITIONS

Fatemi, Falon. "The True Cost of a Bad Hire—It's More Than You Think." *Forbes,* Sep 28, 2016. https://www.forbes.com/sites/falonfatemi/2016/09/28/the-true-cost-of-a-bad-hire-its-more-than-you-think/?sh=12f6dbe4aa41.

Favaro, Ken, Per-Ola Karlsson, and Gary L. Neilson. "The $112 Billion CEO Succession Problem." *Strategy+Business,* May 2015. https://www.strategy-business.com/article/00327.

Deloitte, LLP. *Your Guide: Directors' Remuneration in FTSE 100 Companies.* London: CoRe Creative Services, 2020.

Development Dimensions International. *Leadership Transitions Report 2021.* Bridgeville: Development Dimensions International, May 19th, 2021. https://www.ddiworld.com/research/leadership-transitions-report.

Isaac, Mike. "Uber Founder Travis Kalanick Resigns as C.E.O." *New York Times,* June 21, 2017. https://www.nytimes.com/2017/03/08/technology/snap-makes-a-bet-on-the-cultural-supremacy-of-the-camera.html.

Keller, Scott and Mary Meaney. "Successfully Transitioning to New Leadership Roles." *McKinsey & Company,* May 23, 2018. https://www.veruspartners.net/wp-content/uploads/2018/06/Successfully-transitioning-to-new-leadership-roles-web-final.pdf

Nawaz, Sabina. "The Biggest Mistakes New Executives Make." *Harvard Business Review,* May 15, 2017.

O'Kelley, Rusty and Russell Reynolds Associates. "CEO Transitions: Mitigating Risks and Accelerating Value Creation." *Harvard Law School Forum on Corporate Governance* (blog), December 9, 2018. https://corpgov.law.harvard.edu/2018/12/09/ceo-transitions-mitigating-risks-and-accelerating-value-creation/.

Shekshnia, Stanislav, and Gry Osnes. "Why the Best CEOs Are Already Thinking About Their Exits." *Harvard Business Review,* October 31, 2019. https://hbr.org/2019/10/why-the-best-ceos-are-already-thinking-about-their-exits.

Stoddard, Nat, and Claire Wyckoff. "The Costs of CEO Failure." *Chief Executive,* December 12, 2008. https://chiefexecutive.net/the-costs-of-ceo-failure/.

Wallmine. "Jennifer Morgan Net Worth." Last modified October 1, 2021. https://wallmine.com/nyse/sap/officer/1944243/jennifer-morgan.

Weinmann, Karlee, and Aimee Groth. "The Shortest-Tenured CEOs In History." *Business Insider Australia,* September 24, 2011. https://www.businessinsider.com.au/ceos-short-tenures-2011-9.

Wilson, Denise. *Hampton-Alexander Review: FTSE Women Leaders.* London: FTSE Women Leaders, 2021.

CHAPTER 8—KEY EXECUTIVE TRANSITION CHALLENGES: PEOPLE & CULTURE

Keller, Scott and Mary Meaney. "Successfully Transitioning to New Leadership Roles." *McKinsey & Company,* May 23, 2018. https://www.veruspartners.net/wp-content/uploads/2018/06/Successfully-transitioning-to-new-leadership-roles-web-final.pdf

Sakulku, Jaruwan. "The Impostor Phenomenon." *International Journal of Behavioral Science,* 6, no. 1 (2011): 75-97. https://doi.org/10.14456/ijbs.2011.6

Watkins, Michael D. *Master Your Next Move: Proven Strategies for Navigating the First 90 Days.* Massachusetts: Harvard Business Publishing, 2019.

Watkins, Michael D. *The First 90 Days: Critical Success Strategies for New Leaders at All Levels.* Massachusetts: Harvard Business Publishing, 2003.

CHAPTER 9—KEY EXECUTIVE TRANSITION CHALLENGES: BUSINESS & TECHNICAL

Watkins, Michael D. *Master Your Next Move: The Essential Companion to "The First 90 Days."* Massachusetts: Harvard Business Publishing, 2019.

CHAPTER 10—THE BUSINESS CASE FOR SUCCESSFUL EXECUTIVE TRANSITIONS

Carucci, Ron. "Executives Fail to Execute Strategy Because They're Too Internally Focussed." *Harvard Business Review*, November 13, 2017. https://hbr.org/2017/11/executives-fail-to-execute-strategy-because-theyre-too-internally-focused.

CEB. *High-Impact Leadership Transitions: A Transformative Approach.* Arlington County: The Corporate Executive Board Company, 2012. https://docplayer.net/4194979-High-impact-leadership-transitions-a-transformative-approach.html.

Dineen, Sean. "De-Risking Executive Transitions to Accelerate Value Creation." March 9, 2021. Russell Reynolds and Hunt Scanlon Media. Virtual Webinar, 30:31-30:52. https://huntscanlon.com/webinars/de-risking-executive-transitions-to-accelerate-value-creation/.

Fatemi, Falon. "The True Cost of a Bad Hire—It's More Than You Think." *Forbes,* Sep 28, 2016. https://www.forbes.com/sites/falonfatemi/2016/09/28/the-true-cost-of-a-bad-hire-its-more-than-you-think/?sh=12f6dbe4aa41.

Keller, Scott and Mary Meaney. "Successfully Transitioning to New Leadership Roles." *McKinsey & Company,* May 23, 2018. https://www.veruspartners.net/wp-content/uploads/2018/06/Successfully-transitioning-to-new-leadership-roles-web-final.pdf.

Lombardi, Mollie. *Onboarding 2011: The Path to Productivity.* Boston: Aberdeen Group, 2011. https://www.talentwise.com/files/Onboarding_2011_-_The_Path_to_Productivity.pdf.

Masters, Brooke. "Rise of a Headhunter." *Financial Times,* March 30, 2009. https://www.ft.com/content/19975256-1af2-11de-8aa3-0000779fd2ac.

Nawaz, Sabina. "The Biggest Mistakes New Executives Make." *Harvard Business Review,* May 15, 2017. https://hbr.org/2017/05/the-biggest-mistakes-new-executives-make.

Watkins, Michael D. *How Transition Coaches Accelerate Executive Onboarding.* Lausanne: International Institute for Management Development, 2017.

Wheeler, Patricia. "Senior Leadership Transitions: What Makes Them Work and What Causes Them to Fail?" *Business Coaching Worldwide,* October 2009. https://wabccoaches.com/2009/09/senior-leadership-transitions-what-makes-them-work-and-what-causes-them-to-fail/.

Ulrich, Dave, Norm Smallwood, and Mike Ulrich. "The Leadership Gap." The RBL Group, August 3, 2020. https://www.rbl.net/insights/articles/the-leadership-gap.

CHAPTER 11—KEY INTERVENTIONS FOR SUCCESSFUL EXECUTIVE TRANSITIONS

Bradt, George, Jayme A. Check, and Jorge E. Pedraza. *The New Leader's 100-Day Action Plan: How to Take Charge, Build or Merge Your Team, and Get Immediate Results.* New York, John Wiley & Sons, Inc, 2011.

Burroughs, Michael K. *Before Onboarding: How to Integrate New Leaders for Quick and Sustained Results.* Createspace Independent Publishing Platform, 2011.

Byford, Mark, Michael D. Watkins, and Lena Triantogiannis. "Onboarding Isn't Enough." *Harvard Business Review,* May–June 2017. https://hbr.org/2017/05/onboarding-isnt-enough.

Clutterbuck, David. "Why Line Manager Coaching Often Doesn't Work and What to Do About It" *David Clutterbuck Partnership* (blog), April 12, 2021. https://davidclutterbuckpartnership.com/why-line-manager-coaching-often-doesnt-work-and-what-to-do-about-it/.

Development Dimensions International. *Leadership Transitions Report 2021*. Bridgeville: Development Dimensions International, May 19, 2021. https://www.ddiworld.com/research/leadership-transitions-report.

Davis, Ian. "Letter to a Newly Appointed CEO." *McKinsey & Company,* June 1, 2010. https://www.mckinsey.com/featured-insights/leadership/letter-to-a-newly-appointed-ceo.

Fishman, Anton: "How Interim Managers Transition into New Roles: A Behavioural Investigation of Successful Entry Strategies." Slideshow presented at the First International Conference for Research into Interim Management, formerly Cass Business School (now Bayes Business School),, London, UK, November 2008.

Keller, Scott and Mary Meaney. "Successfully Transitioning to New Leadership Roles." *McKinsey & Company,* May 23, 2018. https://www.veruspartners.net/wp-content/uploads/2018/06/Successfully-transitioning-to-new-leadership-roles-web-final.pdf.

Triantogiannis, Lena, and Mark Byford. "Onboarding Isn't Enough: Executives Need To Be Fully Integrated Into Your Culture." *EgonZehnder,* April 19, 2017. https://www.egonzehnder.com/what-we-do/leadership-advisory/accelerated-integration/insights/onboarding-isnt-enough-executives-need-to-be-fully-integrated-into-your-culture.

Watkins, Michael D. *The First 90 Days: Critical Success Strategies for New Leaders at All Levels.* Massachusetts: Harvard Business Publishing, 2003.

CHAPTER 12—INTRODUCTION TO THE DOUBLE DIAMOND FRAMEWORK© OF EXECUTIVE TRANSITIONS

Dineen, Sean. "De-Risking Executive Transitions to Accelerate Value Creation." March 9, 2021. Russell Reynolds and Hunt Scanlon Media. Virtual Webinar, 23:40. https://huntscanlon.com/webinars/de-risking-executive-transitions-to-accelerate-value-creation/.

Fogg, BJ. "15 Ways Behavior Can Change: Behavior Design Lab at Stanford University." Fogg Behavior Grid. Last modified August 18, 2018. https://www.behaviorgrid.org/.

Gabarro, John J. *The Dynamics of Taking Charge*. Massachusetts: Harvard Business Publishing, 1987.

Gaines, Jeffrey. "The Philosophy of Ikigai: 3 Examples About Finding Purpose." *PositivePsychology.com,* August 24, 2021. https://positivepsychology.com/ikigai/.

Gaines-Ross, Leslie. *CEO Capital: A Guide to Building CEO Reputation and Company Success*. Hoboken: Wiley, 2002.

Hogan Assessments. "Leadership Forecast Series." Products. Last modified October 15, 2015. https://www.hoganassessments.com/products/leadership-forecast-series/.

Perell, David (@david_perell). "The writing process has two phases: Divergence & convergence. In the divergence phase, you playfully explore new ideas. In the convergence phase, you shift into a state of focus where you simplify your ideas so you can publish them. Collect the dots, then connect the dots." Twitter, March 10, 2021). 10:43 a.m. https://twitter.com/david_perell/status/1369690289762414592?s=20.

Savage, Maddy. "Burnout Is Rising in the Land of Work-Life Balance." *BBC: Worklife,* July 26, 2019. https://www.bbc.com/worklife/article/20190719-why-is-burnout-rising-in-the-land-of-work-life-balance.

Schwartz, Tony and Catherine McCarthy. "Manage Your Energy, Not Your Time." *Harvard Business Review,* October 2007. https://hbr.org/2007/10/manage-your-energy-not-your-time.

CHAPTER 13—THE DOUBLE DIAMOND© FRAMEWORK OF EXECUTIVE TRANSITIONS

Dineen, Sean. "De-Risking Executive Transitions to Accelerate Value Creation." March 9, 2021a. Russell Reynolds and Hunt Scanlon Media. Virtual Webinar, 10:30. https://huntscanlon.com/webinars/de-risking-executive-transitions-to-accelerate-value-creation/.

Dineen, Sean. "De-Risking Executive Transitions to Accelerate Value Creation." March 9, 2021b. Russell Reynolds and Hunt Scanlon Media. Virtual Webinar, 17:08. https://huntscanlon.com/webinars/de-risking-executive-transitions-to-accelerate-value-creation/.

Dineen, Sean. "De-Risking Executive Transitions to Accelerate Value Creation." March 9, 2021c. Russell Reynolds and Hunt Scanlon Media. Virtual Webinar, 28:21. https://huntscanlon.com/webinars/de-risking-executive-transitions-to-accelerate-value-creation/.

Marshall, Ernest. "Webinar: Succeeding in HR: Advice from Recently Appointed CHROs." December 4, 2020. Russell Reynolds Associates. Virtual Webinar, 9:19. https://www.youtube.com/watch?v=EKGyHIEeM5o.

Myszkowski, Gary J. *Senior Executive Transitions: Managing the Three Waves of Change.* Hudson: Executive Core, 2014.

O'Keeffe, Niamh. *Your First 100 Days: Make Maximum Impact in Your New Role.* New Jersey: Pearson Education, 2011.

Pratt, Mary K. "New CIOs: How to succeed in the first 120 days." SearchCIO, August 21, 2015. https://searchcio.techtarget.com/tip/New-CIOs-How-to-succeed-in-the-first-120-days.

Pritchard, Kathryn. "Webinar: Succeeding in HR: Advice from Recently Appointed CHROs." December 4, 2020a. Russell Reynolds Associates. Virtual Webinar, 4:55. https://www.youtube.com/watch?v=EKGyHIEeM5o.

Pritchard, Kathryn. "Webinar: Succeeding in HR: Advice from Recently Appointed CHROs." December 4, 2020b. Russell Reynolds Associates. Virtual Webinar, 7:29. https://www.youtube.com/watch?v=EKGyHIEeM5o.

Schmidt, Erik. "Webinar: Succeeding in HR: Advice from Recently Appointed CHROs." December 4, 2020. Russell Reynolds Associates. Virtual Webinar, 44:54. https://www.youtube.com/watch?v=EKGyHIEeM5o.

St. Leger, Tina. "Webinar: Succeeding in HR: Advice from Recently Appointed CHROs." December 4, 2020. Russell Reynolds Associates. Virtual Webinar, 16:36. https://www.youtube.com/watch?v=EKGyHIEeM5o.

CHAPTER 14—HOW TO SUCCESSFULLY TRANSITION OUT OF AN EXECUTIVE ROLE

Caspar, Christian, and Michael Halbye. "Making the Most of the CEO's Last 100 Days." *McKinsey & Company*, January 1, 2011. https://www.mckinsey.com/featured-insights/leadership/making-the-most-of-the-ceos-last-100-days.

Citrin, James M., Claudius A. Hildebrand, and Robert J. Stark. "The CEO Life Cycle." *Harvard Business Review*, November-December 2019. https://hbr.org/2019/11/the-ceo-life-cycle.

Dammann, Angelika. "SAP HR Leader Leaves after Criticism about Using the Corporate Jet" (translated from German). Der Spiegel, July 8, 2011. https://www.spiegel.de/wirtschaft/unternehmen/angelika-dammann-sap-personalchefin-geht-nach-firmenjet-kritik-a-773234.html.

Dineen, Sean. "De-Risking Executive Transitions to Accelerate Value Creation." March 9, 2021a. Russell Reynolds and Hunt Scanlon Media. Virtual Webinar, 21:25. https://huntscanlon. com/webinars/de-risking-executive-transitions-to-acceler-ate-value-creation/.

George, Bill. "The CEO's Guide to Retirement." *Harvard Business Review*, November-December 2019. https://hbr.org/2019/11/the-ceos-guide-to-retirement.

Hebbelinck, Trui. "Webinar: Succeeding in HR: Advice from Recently Appointed CHROs." December 4, 2020. Russell Reynolds Associates. Virtual Webinar, 13:21. https://www.youtube. com/watch?v=EKGyHIEeM50.

O'Kelley, Rusty and Russell Reynolds Associates. "CEO Transitions: Mitigating Risks and Accelerating Value Creation." *Harvard Law School Forum on Corporate Governance* (blog), December 9, 2018. https://corpgov.law.harvard.edu/2018/12/09/ceo-transitions-mitigating-risks-and-accelerating-value-creation/.

ACKNOWLEDGMENTS

First and foremost, I would like to thank all of my contributors and the executives for sharing their wisdom, expertise, and personal stories with me. You have given me what is your most valuable asset: Your time and embodied executive experience. Your sharing has been invaluable to this body of work and will be as inspiring to the readers as it was to me personally and professionally. I have had the immense privilege of interviewing a stellar cast of executives including:

Anton Fishman (Mentor & Director)
Dr. Brian Underhill (CEO & Coach)
Erik Schmidt (CHRO)
Dr. Hannes Ametsreiter (CEO)
Michael K. Burroughs (President & Coach)
Richard Demblon (CHRO)
Rudi Kindts (Mentor, CHRO & Coach)

I would also like to gratefully acknowledge early supporters of my book by contributing to the pre-launch campaign:

Abolfazl Kakaei, Adam Akbar, Alan Wilson, Alireza Soltany Noory, Dr. Andreas Jacobsen, Andrew Dyckhoff, Andrew Pryde, Angela Zinser, Anniek Kindts, Anton Fishman, Arron Smith, Marcello Maggioni, Behdad Naziri, Belash Bagherian, Birgit Hoffmann, Dr. Brian Underhill, Bridget Goona, Burcu Ozenli, Carla Picolli, Carol Braddick, Catherine Blaikie, Chris Breeze, Christian Alberti, Claire Bennett, Claudia Jorde, Corinne Williams, Craig O'Flaherty, Damian Siggins, Daniel Ahlers, Daniel Lukas Rau, David Corran, David Sparling, David Whan, Devi Selliappan-Anne, Edward Lamont, Ehsan Arasteh, Prof. Dr. Eric Koester, Erik Schmidt, Esra Canderler, Fatih Subasi, Florian Bosch, Gary Brown, Gavin Epstein, Georgi Vasilev, Giovanni Giordano, Govinda Sateesh Kamath, Grace Thomas, Graeme Thompson, Hamidreza Lachin, HanhLinh HoTran, Helen Cottle, Inke Schulze-Seeger, Jafar Bolouk Azari, Jan Holzberg, Janine Ahlers , Jeremy Sutton, Jimmy Garnier, John Wegman, Jordan Archer, Juliette Aucamp, Dr. Keith Amoss, Kristina Schinz, Lan Anh Salzer, Leslie Rance, Linda Ullrich, Martin Giese, Marinela Tanase, Mark Watson, Martin MC Brown, Matthew Johnson, Mohsen Moradi Moghadam, Morad Sajasi, Nigel Toon, Nils De Rop, Osman Peermamode, Philip Lacor, Rebecca Hone, Riddhima Kowley, Rudi Kindts, Sabine Erber-Hass, Saeed Aliasgari, Sanika Rathod, Sara Rezaeian, Schaahin Azizi, Sergey Kochergan, Sharam Sadeghi, Shekhar Datta, Shirin Rayga, Sudhersan Ramasamy, Tamara Ahlers, Terry Hoffmann, Thomas Guy, Tom Birch, Traci Hughes, Vivien Yao, Will Wigmore, Yoosuf Moiz, Dr. Zain Reddiar, Zsofia Juhasz

Furthermore, I would like to thank my publisher New Degree Press and the various colleagues who have supported this book with developmental editing, marketing, and acquisitions revisions, cover design, copy editing, heavy pen reading and feedback, and so much more.

Last but not least, my gratitude goes to Professor Eric Koester, PhD who has been a great guide and a source of energy and inspiration.

All of you have helped me share this body of work with a wide range of executives.

If you do have any comments, feedback, or questions, do get in touch via:

hello@masteringexecutivetransitions.com or visit www.masteringexecutivetransitions.com

Made in the USA
Columbia, SC
08 August 2024

40132245R00133